Soaring –
A Teen's Guide to
Spirit and Spirituality

Soaring –
A Teen's Guide to
Spirit and Spirituality

Deneen Vukelic

Winchester, UK
Washington, USA

First published by Soul Rocks Books, 2015
Soul Rocks Books is an imprint of John Hunt Publishing Ltd., Laurel House, Station Approach,
Alresford, Hants, SO24 9JH, UK
office1@jhpbooks.net
www.johnhuntpublishing.com
www.soulrocks-books.com

For distributor details and how to order please visit the 'Ordering' section on our website.

Text copyright: Deneen Vukelic 2014

ISBN: 978 1 78279 874 3
Library of Congress Control Number: 2014951067

A CIP catalogue record for this book is available from the British Library.

Design: Lee Nash

Printed and bound by CPI Group (UK) Ltd, Croydon, CR0 4YY

We operate a distinctive and ethical publishing philosophy in all
areas of our business, from our global network of authors to
production and worldwide distribution.

CONTENTS

(In Order of Appearance in my Life)
I dedicate this book to:

My Mom
Who has taught me more about unconditional love than any other
person I know.

Sasha, My Husband
Who, when I informed him that I was writing a book didn't look at me
like I was crazy, but instead gave me all his love and support without
question.

My Three Sons
Luca
Who inspires me to be a better mother with his kind heart and gentle
presence.
Gabriel
Who teaches me every single day about love and loving.
Julian
Who is my healer and who has taught me so much about love and
patience.

Note to the reader: The healing section of this book is intended as an informational guide. The remedies, holistic healing approaches and techniques described herein are meant to supplement, and not to be a substitute for, professional medical care or treatment. They should not be used to treat a serious ailment without prior consultation with a qualified healthcare professional.

Acknowledgements

The biggest acknowledgement goes to my loving husband of 18 years, Sasha. He has supported me in all my endeavors, on this spiritual journey that began when motherhood began for me. He is my biggest supporter and the person who grounds me when I get too lost in the clouds. I'm truly blessed to have him as my anchor and champion. My most heartfelt thanks goes to him. Also, to my three sons, Luca, Gabriel and Julian, who teach me about motherhood every single day. They are the inspiration for everything I do. I love them dearly.

A special thanks to my two best friends and fellow spiritual pioneers, Carmel Malone Quane and Esther Jimenez. Both of whom have brought so much richness, love and support in my life every day. They too, are my healers, spiritual co-pilots and the dearest of friends. I feel blessed to have them in my life.

A special thanks to three of my young teenage readers. Lidiana, Tara and Sarah. It's beautiful young women like you who bring so much love and light to all. Your support, guidance and enthusiasm in the process of writing this book was much appreciated.

There are so many people in my life who support me in various ways that I am unable to list them all, but I hope you know who you are and how much you mean to me.

Last, but most definitely not least, I want to acknowledge the loving support I receive from my spiritual teachers – the ascended masters, angels and spirit guides who brought me along this path, and who intuitively inspired me to write a book for teens, and then guided me in the writing of it. I'm particularly grateful for the Beloved Ascended Master Saint Germain whose presence became known to me the summer of 2013, and it is because of him with his loving support and guidance that this book even exists. I'm so thankful that I listened. Thank you to all my beloved masters and teachers for all that you give to me each and every day.

Introduction

Writing this book has been a labor of love. A love and desire to serve the next generation of human beings to be the best, most successful, loving and joyful spirits that they can be; that is my purpose and goal. The world is quite troubled right now, and we need the loving and high vibrations of today's children and teenagers to help humanity lift and raise itself into the next loving dimensions.

I became a holistic healing practitioner after having my three children. My spiritual and healing journey began when I was planning to have my third child. Becoming a mother changed everything I knew about myself. The responsibility in raising my children to be conscious, moral, loving and happy adults was of the utmost importance to me. But, helping only my children wasn't enough. My intuition told me that I was needed to help all children.

After securing my place as a holistic healing practitioner, I created a spiritual workshop program with the help of my personal spiritual support system in order to help children develop their intuition and learn how to meditate. Developing one's intuition empowers an individual in ways no other psychological tool will, because when you feel the spiritual connection and loving vibrations of those Beings in the spiritual realm, nothing will make you feel more supported and less alone. My classes were for the children ages 10 to 12 and 7-9 years of age. It was tremendously gratifying to see my students meditate and share their experiences in the class. My own children participated in their respective class levels and I enjoyed watching them develop and grow as well.

Several years have passed, and these same kids are now teenagers. As I watch and observe their changes and transitions, and listen to the stories about their peers and experiences at school and socially, it is becoming apparent to me that teens need some spiritual guidance and support. Whether it's cool or not to seek out God and develop your spirituality is between you and God and is deeply personal. My feeling is that everyone in your generation is realizing that it *is* cool to talk to God and develop a personal relationship with angels, spirit guides, ascended masters, etc. It's my feeling as well, that there are a lot more of you than you realize reaching for spiritual knowledge because of a deep yearning inside telling you definitely that there's more than you've been taught…much, much more. So, in working with my spiritual support team, I was guided to reach beyond my small community of kids and teens. That's when it came to me that I should write this book.

All of the books and literature out there that talk about spirituality, God and the divine path are written for adults. The handful of books that are written specifically for teens are helpful, but from the kids and teenagers I've been working with, there didn't seem to be enough of the kind of information they were looking for. This book can be considered a beginner's guide on spirituality. It can be used to fill in the blanks of your existing knowledge if you've already begun this journey; or it can be a whole new resource for developing your spirituality, self-confidence, clarity and focus towards your life purpose. It also offers supportive guidance for handling your everyday life.

Be aware that this book will go deeper and further than any religious education you might have had. It does not matter if you were raised Catholic, Jewish, Protestant, Muslim, Hindu, Mormon, etc., or with nothing at all; this is a book about the spiritual path, not a religious path. You chose this book because you were guided to read it. It was written for you in this life stage. It provides information, guidance, tools and examples that relate to your life as a teen or college student.

There are a lot of amazing things going on in and around the planet. No doubt you might have felt these changes, if not directly then most definitely on a subconscious level. Perhaps you have already noticed you are intuitive, "psychic," or sensitive in some way. You are probably a natural born healer as well if you if you aren't aware of that fact. I'm not surprised. Many kids born from the late 1990s to present are genetically different to previous generations. I'm sure your parents are intrigued by the fact that you can fix and navigate their technology devices without prior knowledge. Even my seven-year-old son, who when he was two, programmed his voice to be the ring tone on my cell phone. I didn't even know the phone had that feature, and it took a while for me to figure out how he did this.

Your generation is also amazingly gifted. You all carry a lot of light and higher vibrations than your predecessors because you all came into this world to raise the vibration and collectively help the planet heal. You are gifted but need a GPS system to navigate this world and the world of spirit. I hope this book will become that guidance system for you – guiding you on to the path that leads back to love, to peace, to joy, to God.

The earth is in turmoil now – turmoil that's ultimately for the greater good, but earth and humanity need your help, and I see that you need training and guidance to be that help. Your desire to read this book and connect to God and spiritual beings is because you know you have work to do in helping to raise the vibrations of humanity and the planet. Our oceans and lands are polluted; our food is produced with chemicals and over processed, our animals are raised inhumanely. There is war, terrorism, greed, and anger driving our governments worldwide. Humanity needs your beautiful souls to bring light to earth. Your service will bring you further along your own divine path towards purity, joy and unconditional love and harmony while at the same time assisting earth and humanity towards its own light and divinity.

In reading this book, each chapter builds on the previous

chapter, so I do suggest you read in order. Your understanding of everything will be more thorough if you read all of it. But, if it's your nature to skip around, you can do this as well. Each section is complete in and of itself.

I wish you many blessings of joy, light, abundance, love and success on your journey and I thank you for allowing me to be a part of it. Read on!

Part I

The Basics

Chapter I

God and You: We Are All One

What is God? Who is God? Is God a She? Is God a He? Is God in me? These questions you may have asked yourself at some point in your life since you were very little; since you received religious instructions. The simple answer is, You Are God and God is You. Okay, what does that mean? Well, from every piece of spiritual literature, teachings and trainings I've received, the simple fact is that we are all one. I'm sure you have heard this, but you still ask, "but what does that mean?" This means we are individual beings of God. We have our human personality, human ego, but our human self is connected to our true self which is our God-Self. Our God-Self is connected to the God Source of which every being in the universe is connected. Our soul, when it's released from our bodies at death, merges back into the God Source. Telepathically, intuitively, and spiritually we are always connected to God. We are never not connected to God. For the purposes of clarity and to differentiate from our God-Selves, I'm using the term "God Source" to indicate what we understand to be as God. Each of us, though, is an individual being of the God Source clothed in a human body attached to our God-Self. Later in this chapter, I will be teaching you a new term for God-Self which is quite beautiful.

Most of us as children and adults through attending religious services at our family's place of worship are taught in a way that makes God feel he is above us, but not actually part of us. Like he is a benevolent grandfather in a white robe and white beard always looking after us from Heaven. While it's beautiful to know and feel his loving light and radiation showering us when we tune in, that's always felt so far away to me. If you are Christian, you are taught that Jesus was God's son. He lived and died for us, but after his Ascension which we celebrate every Easter, he too, feels apart and far away from us living in Heaven. If you are Jewish, Muslim or other Christian faiths, you may pray to saints, prophets, or angels. Again, these beautiful Beings are "in Heaven" with God; always seeming to be so far away from us. Do you feel like you are left alone or isolated with this kind of understanding? Religion teaches only one way to feel somewhat closer to God, Jesus, the saints or prophets and that is by prayer and attending services in a place of worship. I'm pleased to tell you it's so much more than that — that the Spiritual Heavenly realm is much closer, and we can connect in ways you never thought were possible. It's so much closer and more wonderful than you realize. If your parents have already taught you a more expansive way to view God and your spirituality, then my hat's off to them. This book will resonate with them as well, even though it's written with you, dear readers, in mind.

As I mentioned in my introduction, I will be straying from what is traditionally taught in churches, temples, religious books and teachings. But if you are reading this book, then I think you are already highly sensitive enough to understand spirituality at this level. You are already asking the big questions about your existence, your place in the universe, and sense that there is much more than you have ever imagined. This means you are ready for what is written in this book.

In keeping with the theme of this chapter, I would like to introduce you to new terminology that will explain how you are connected to God. Connected to every human being on this planet is our own, individual, Beloved 'Mighty I AM Presence.'® The 'I AM Presence' is your God-Self and from here on I will use both terms, God-Self or 'I AM Presence,' or 'Presence' for short.

Your Beloved 'Mighty I AM Presence' is your true self, your soul. To be close to God is through connecting daily with your God-Self; your 'I AM Presence.' Your 'Presence' knows everything you need to get along in this lifetime. [*This unique*

4

expression,'Mighty I AM Presence,' was created by the Ascended Master Saint Germain for His Students. In It He embedded the Great Creative Word, 'I AM.' It is used in this book 'The Magic Presence'®️ by permission of the Saint Germain Foundation.®️] If you cultivate a relationship with this part of you, it will guide, teach, love and protect you in powerful ways. It is *already* doing this for you, but once you begin to connect with this true part of yourself, it will provide for you in ways you didn't think was possible from the vantage point of your human ego and personality.

Let me explain further. As I mentioned, every human being is connected to their soul, their God-Self. You are connected to this part of you through a silver cord which doesn't disconnect until your death when your soul, your being-ness, merges back to God. During your lifetime, depending on the quality of your heart, and level of your humanity, your 'Presence' can be anywhere from twelve feet above you to much higher – as much as fifty feet or more. The goal here is to bring your 'Presence' in as close to your physical body as possible until you can merge with your 'Presence.' This is what they call the Ascension. To do that our physical, mental and emotional bodies must be pure and cleared of all negativity and past negative deeds and thoughts. By beginning the work of connecting with your 'I AM Presence,' you will begin to bridge that distance. All answers about your reason for being here, your divine path, your divine purpose, your service to humanity, who or if you will marry, have children, where you will live, is controlled and guided by your Beloved 'Mighty I AM Presence.' This part of you is already guiding you in many different ways. If you are an intuitive or a highly sensitive person, you may be aware of taking advantage of this guidance by following your instincts, following your intuition. That is excellent. If you are reading this book, you have been guided to do so as well. Of that I am certain.

The goal of every student of spirit should be to attain perfection. I know that this would seem an impossible task, but it's not. By simply setting this intention and beginning the work, you will quickly feel positive changes within yourself. For instance, you will have moments of joy just for being. The joy won't be connected to the new thing you purchased, or the special occasion you experienced, or a good grade or report card, and so on, but you will feel joyous just doing your everyday activities like going to school, doing homework, helping out your parents, going to work, and similar. You will also feel shifts in your perceptions about people. You might feel less defensive in an angry situation. You will begin to feel compassion for cranky, angry or unpleasant people, and not react to their negativity or behavior. You might begin to feel like old hurts and negative emotional memories begin to clear away and heal. As you continue on this path of meditation, purifying, and being a kind, loving, peaceful and compassionate person, you will also begin to connect with what you are supposed to be doing – not only the big-picture stuff, like which classes you should take, or what major in college you want to go for, but everyday stuff, like helping your neighbor shovel snow, or bringing in the groceries for your mother, or babysitting your siblings without expecting payment so your mom and dad can have a date night. As your sensitivity begins to open, you will be guided in everything single thing, from the smallest, like giving someone at the super-market a smile to brighten their day, to what leisure activity you wish to enjoy on Friday night – whatever it is it will always be the right thing you should be doing at that moment.

It's a process, a long and wonderful journey that just gets better and better and better. You will have bumpy and grumpy days, and days where you feel totally disconnected from your God-Self, but getting back on track is part of the learning. You will find that love heals and transforms everything. I mean every-thing! You want to fix your relationship with your parents, use love. Apologize first *and* sincerely. You'd be surprised how quickly the situation will turn around if you approach everything with compassion and the feeling of love.

The key to a harmonious life, loving and supportive relationships, positive outcomes, happy experiences is positive intention. If your words are positive, but the emotions behind them are negative or you just don't believe the words you are saying, your emotions will determine the outcome no matter how many times you recite positive affirmations. You must do and say everything you want with *true feeling*. As you learn this, as you clear yourself of past karma and negative patterns, it will become easier and what you positively request in your life will come sooner or faster. It's important to stay consistent and persistent. You will find that once you are on this path, there's no going back. You will miss your connection to your Beloved 'Presence.' You will miss the little miracles, the sweet joyful moments, and good feelings that began to be part of your everyday life. This is a one-way trip to all you can imagine and dream for yourself.

Your 'I AM Presence' is also your source for all abundance, and supply. As you tune in, and begin to work and connect with your God-Self, what you want will manifest in your life. There will be a momentum and things will happen that you didn't ask for but enjoy because you created an energetic momentum to attract all that's positive. I'll give you a brief example. Two days ago, I receive a phone call from my cell-phone service provider. When the caller identified hmself on the telephone, I was a little surprised. Usually these calls are to collect on a past due bill. Instead I was pleasantly surprised to find that this service representative wanted to tell me that the company was lowering my bill by $15 because they had a new plan offering the same service I already had, but was now cheaper than I had been paying. I was pleasantly stunned. This is an example of when you live with your God-Self in charge as much as possible; you attract positivity, and abundance in all forms. Allow the universe to provide for you in clever, unusual and convoluted ways. It's fun to watch how things unfold for you and it shows how interestingly we are all connected.

Before I close this chapter, I'd like to briefly talk about gratitude. Gratitude is one of the most powerful emotions to raise your vibration, increase the amount of divine love and light in your body, mind and feeling to bring you closer to union with God. In everything you do, every person you meet or interact with, every job, chore or activity you do, be grateful. Be grateful to your God-Self. Be grateful to your parents, siblings, extended family, friends, teachers, acquaintances, peers, strangers and even those you perceive as enemies. In every moment of every day, we are both teachers and students of life and life lessons. Enemies, by the way, can be our greatest teachers. What we gain from these types of lessons is determined by our level of understanding of love and forgiveness. Forgiveness being the key to learning and overcoming the lesson no matter how hard they are at the time. Be grateful to be alive each morning and feel the joy of being alive no matter what your home life is. Each day is a new opportunity to do better, to feel and find happiness, contentment, peace, joy and love. Nothing is a foregone conclusion. If you want a better life, be first grateful for what you already have. And if you feel you have nothing and no one, just be simply grateful to be alive and to have another opportunity to achieve or manifest what you want.

In closing this chapter, I'd like to add some personal comments about my use and reference to *The Magic Presence* throughout Part I of this book. It was written in 1935 and is a story – a romantic story in truth – of four teenagers who because of their advance level of spirituality were permitted to work directly with Saint Germain and many other ascended masters in preparation for their ascension at this tender young age. It was and still is quite rare for someone so young to be born at a level that is advanced enough for this special privilege. I chose this book for many,

many reasons, including the most obvious one that this book is about four individuals who are around your age. It is included in the recommended books listed at the back, but it seemed important to mention in detail here. I do hope you will feel encouraged to purchase a copy of this extraordinary book to read and learn spiritual lessons that are far wiser and more relevant than many books and sources out there today. Lastly, in addition to the wonderful story and spiritual lessons of *The Magic Presence*, there is also a radiation that comes to you when reading the book that is truly loving peaceful and even healing. You can't help but feel it as you read through the pages of this amazing and true story.

Chapter 2

Understanding Intuition:
Learn All the Ways it Works

What is intuition? Here is the dictionary definition:

> Intuition – n 1. Direct perception of truth, fact, etc. independent of any reasoning process; immediate apprehension. 2. A fact or truth, etc. perceived this way. 3. A keen or quick insight. 4. The quality or ability to have direct perception or keen insight.

Simply put, intuition is knowing something with some certainty without knowing why you know it. We all have intuitive abilities. You have been using yours since you were a baby. This ability is within each human being. But what is not developed in many of us is the ability to recognize it at work. I'm sure you have had many "gut instincts" or a strong feeling of "knowing" which is definitely your intuition working. But noticing when your intuition is at work for all things big and small is the other piece of it that many people do not know how to recognize and take advantage of. The key is in tuning in to your sixth sense – your inner guidance which can be coming from your God-Self, or through your spirit guides, angels, etc., depending on what the information is that you need in a given moment.

If you are reading this book, I sense that your intuition is more developed than others in your age group. I've read, and am seeing in your generation and those younger being born with high levels of sensitivity, intuitive abilities, and a strong connection to God and your spirituality. You all carry more light, higher vibrations, which means you are naturally able to connect to God and many, different types of Light Beings in the Heavenly realms more easily than you parents' generation. You might recall when you were very little the ability to see people's auras, or see or sense when there was "an energy" in the room; such as deceased relatives, angels, spirit guides, and other benevolent energies.

You may also be naturally sensitive to human energies. Ask yourself: Do you pick up on people's emotional states, worry, sadness, anger, depression, frustration, confusion? Are you able to shrug it off, or does it get stuck to you for a while? Can you easily sense someone's goodness or meanness? This is all part of the package of having the gifts of sensitivity, and intuitive abilities. All wonderful gifts to enjoy once you know and learn how to use them. When you don't know how to use them, these gifts can feel overwhelming and can hinder you tremendously in getting along in the world around you. I hope those that are reading this book have had loving support at home, that it felt safe, and secure – particularly through your parental relationships. If you do not feel that way, there will be tools in this book to assist you in feeling unconditional love, personal safety and inner peace. You are indeed, loved, valued and important to yourself, to humanity and to God. And, you are *never* alone. If you are experiencing an unpleasant childhood and young adulthood right now, be aware that these situations are part of your life lessons. Learning from these relationships and experiences will allow you to heal and grow emotionally and spiritually. In Part II of this book, I will be talking about divine purpose and soul contracts. This might help ease your mind and feelings as you navigate your teens into your early twenties with a new perception on how to view your unpleasant family life and heal yourself in the process.

Recognizing the Different Ways Intuition Comes Through Our Being

Okay, you know you are naturally sensitive and gifted intuitively. I'm going to show you the many ways intuition comes through and give you some fun exercises to develop it further. If you think you have already mastered your intuition and psychic abilities, you can still learn from these seemingly basic tools. It's like someone having a beautiful voice naturally. They will still need voice lessons to develop good breathing, exercises for developing technique, and they will need to practice in order to bring out their ability to interpret a song's lyrics, through artistry. So, even though you are more advanced than some of your peers, this book can assist you in honing and fine-tuning your abilities while providing information about who you are reaching through those invisible connections. I still go back to the basics even though I'm an advanced student of spirit. It's like taking a refresher course reminding us of little things we might have forgotten along the way. Here is a list of five ways to utilize your intuitive senses:

Clairvoyance or "clear seeing" – Many of you may be aware of this term. Clairvoyance is not just the ability to see energy, spirits or auras directly with your eyes. It can also be through your mind's eye. You may be able to see pictures, scenes, words, colors, symbols, movies simply by closing your eyes and seeing through your mind's eye. Some people are born with this gift, as they have a very specific divine purpose and path in which they are meant to use this gift. For all others including myself, we can develop this gift and also learn the language of the pictures, words or images we already might see. It's about interpreting what you receive if it's not clearly illustrated through clairvoyance. I will tell you, that clairvoyance is not my strongest intuitive sense, but I do see colors, words and blurry images. Through guided visualization you can also develop this skill.

Clairaudience – This is the ability to hear your intuitive messages. It can come through as a whisper in your ear like someone's behind you whispering, or it can come through like an inner mind voice. I've only received a couple of intuitive messages this way. It was mostly because my guides and ascended master teachers weren't able to reach me any other way. You're not crazy if you hear voices in your head unless those voices are telling you to murder someone. Then…I'd be a little concerned. Mostly these voices are telling you supportive and loving information to keep you on your divine path.

Clairsentience or "clear feeling" – This is one of the most accessible ways to utilize and tune in to your intuition. Everyone has physical sensations. Have you ever gotten a shiver down your back when you said aloud to someone, some fact or truth about a situation? It's a validation that you are on the right track. Physical sensations can come in many forms, a flutter or stronger heartbeat, a gut feeling, a pain or tingling somewhere in your body, a quick stab of pain in your head, an itch, a twitch. Each signal tells its own type of infor-mation. When you receive a body signal that seems odd to you because it's an isolated sensation, or even a repetitive sensation that doesn't connect to any physical injury of illness, take a moment to tune in and ask what this relates to. It could be information about paying attention to the energy of the person you might be talking to. It could be telling you something to prevent an accident, to let you know of a loved one who might need you, or it could confirming a thought you might have had as validation of being true or indicate you are on the right track. As an energy healer, this is an important sense for me to utilize and I still enjoy fine-tuning it and developing it even further.

Inner Knowing – This is intuition that just appears in your brain as thoughts. If you've tuned in and asked for guidance, suggestions, answers or information, it can appear in your thoughts as a certainty. It's similar to having an inner conver-sation with yourself. You ask questions and your higher self answers in thought form. You can ask the same question a few times and see if the answer stays the same, or keeps giving you the same response. This form of intuitive development is excellent to journal. You can write questions to important and minor issues or concerns, and then tune in and just write what comes to mind. There are a couple of rules or suggestions when choosing this route. First, make sure you make a prayer or decree to receive answers only from the highest spiritual level, or from the ascended master level. You can even be more specific than that. You can ask for assistance from your spirit guide, your 'I AM Presence,' or a specific ascended master. It's important that you do this prior to journaling for guidance, particularly with important issues and situations in your life. You do not want to attract troubled spirits, or beings in the astral level. Many are benevolent, but many are still earthbound and will not offer you guidance that is purely the most loving and beneficial for you. We will discuss more on staying away from the astral level or consciousness later in the book.

Mixed Sensing – This is intuitive guidance received through a combination of senses. Perhaps you received a visual symbol or message, and then felt goose bumps down your back. Or, for example, you can sense physically an answer or guidance that will also be combined with inner knowing through your thoughts. It could be any combination of feelings and sensations...all working to validate or confirm what you think or feel is your answer or guidance.

In summary, this is an opportunity to begin to be aware of any subtle nuance within your body. It's constantly giving you information whether you tune in or not; whether you notice or not. Consider purchasing a journal, and begin writing. If you do not want to constantly write your feelings, you may just want to keep a log of your life questions and the intuitive answers you receive.

Always put the date, and keep track and note when your answers are accurate. You will find that you will get more comfortable with trusting your guidance which will, in turn, improve your accuracy. Journaling keeps a record so you can see the three "P's," patterns, progress and your path. When selecting a journal, choose a style or color that suits your personality so you feel drawn to write in it. You may also want to log important dreams in this same journal. Dreams have their own symbols, messages and intuitive guidance. Learning to write down your dreams will open your mind to being better able to interpret them. This next chapter is another way of working with your intuition and recognizing spiritual guidance when it appears or has been requested by you.

At the back of this book will be meditations and visualizations to use to develop your ability more deeply. But here is a fun activity you can do by yourself or with friends.

Exercise:
Intuitive Game – gather a bunch of color construction papers in: blue, green, yellow, purple, orange and red. Cut them up into squares or rectangles and put in individual opaque envelopes. The 6"x9" envelopes with the metal clasp are excellent for this. Do not label the envelopes. Mix them up and randomly pick one up and feel or see the color or name of the color in your mind's eye, or see if a thought of the color pops into your brain, and then sense a physical sensation to confirm. This is fun to do with friends, but you can do this on your own. Each time you guess the color correctly, take one of the squares out. After several rounds, each person can count up how many squares they collected.

Synchronicity – What It Is and How to Recognize It Working

What is synchronicity? This term was created by the famous psychologist, Carl Gustav Jung, from Austria, who was one of the founders of the study and application of psychology and psychotherapy in the early part of the twentieth century. He had a brilliant mind, was very open to spirituality and was a pioneer in many areas of psychology that drew from his spiritual life. Jung coined the term "synchronicity" as what he considered "meaningful coincidence." In this way of thinking, it describes a type of coincidence that is giving us a message from the universe that relates to what we need to know in that particular time. It could be a reflection of a pattern of thought or thoughts you are having in a given moment or, it can be an answer to a question you had on your mind and sought the universe to provide you with the answer. Not knowing when you will receive the answer but being open to recognizing it when it happens is synchronicity.

This type of natural phenomena ties in nicely with using your various intuitive processes as described in this chapter. The universe is an intricate, complex and seriously clever system through which God, your spirit guides, angels, ascended masters and many other high-octave spiritual beings help communicate to humans on earth. In addition to providing us with clever ways in answering our questions or confirming a thought process or solution, synchronicity can also assist in keeping us on our divine path and purpose, much like a computer's course correction would do on a rocketship or jet plane.

How does one take advantage of this wonderful tool of communication? The answer is many different ways. Perhaps there's a question or a problem you are mentally wrestling with in your mind. You turn on the radio and the first words you hear provide insight into a solution towards solving the problem. Maybe you are indecisive about a certain direction to take, what course of study to choose, whether or not you participate in the school drama club, sports, social activity. Then you read a bumper sticker while driving or riding in a car that gives you an answer. On another occasion you are trying to decide on the character or trustworthiness of an individual, peer or acquaintance. You have a gut feeling, but need confirmation. You may hear a television commercial or program that mimics your gut feelings about the person. There's your answer. This is the direct way of utilizing synchronicity.

Indirectly is another way synchronicity works that resembles more of what coincidence looks like. For example, perhaps you received a school assignment in science, social studies or any particular subject and you need to begin researching the topic. That night on television, you stumble on a documentary for that very, specific topic. Then, the next day, you go to the library, and there's a book on display that also features that subject. Your mother introduces you to a parent she knows through your brother's school who happens to be a professional in the field of study you need to write about. These are just different examples of synchronicity that happen without your question posed to the universe.

A few years ago, I had an argument with a friend, and I was extremely sad and bewildered by the negative outburst from her. As I was driving home later that day, on a car in front of me was a bumper sticker that said "THERE ARE ANGELS ALL AROUND YOU." I immediately felt comforted and able to handle whatever came after and most importantly I didn't feel alone.

So, I say to you, no more offhand comments like, "oh, it's just a coincidence." Yes, it *still* is a coincidence but that "coincidence" may be giving you a message. Stay alert and be mindful…not just to the messages you receive to answers you are seeking, but to all messages. See if they match your thoughts. You never know what you'll need to know.

Chapter 3

Free Will: Understanding What It Is and Why We Have It

As far as I know, every religion recognizes Free Will. It's our God-given right to make our own choices without interference. If beings in the spiritual realm interfered with us without our permission, it could also be disastrous. We must want and be ready for what they have to give or it will not have the intended benefit of bringing in unconditional love, joy, peace, healing and harmony. If they force onto humanity their assistance, or healing without being asked, it could very well be misunderstood and harm not only themselves, but others as well depending on what we were given without them being asked.

Truly, we should look at "Free Will" as a gift from God. We get to make our own choices, even if our guides are suggesting a different choice. There are always consequences for every choice or decision we make – good or bad.

Now, let's talk about Free Will and its application. As you begin using your intuitive tools, and begin to see, feel or "know" your guidance, it may be telling you something that you don't feel inclined to do. Perhaps, it's lack of trust, because your guidance is telling you to do something out of the ordinary, or out of your comfort zone. You may also resist because you don't feel like it's something you want to do. So, you can choose not to listen to your guidance and do something different. I can tell you from experience your 'God-Self,' your guides, and angels truly know what's best for you. Always following their guidance usually means the best opportunities for you. Opportunities for healing, for advancement, for abundance can come in ways that seem incomprehensible to us on earth because of the often convoluted way requests and prayers are answered. Trusting that there's a bigger picture that you can't see and following your inner guidance is always the best course of action. Remember, you already learned about the many ways intuition enters our field of energy – seeing, hearing, sensing, knowing, as well as through synchronicity. You have everything you need to receive, validate and ultimately trust what your communication is. It's taking the leap of faith to act on it. Do not worry if you hesitate too long. Often the universe has a way of opening the path to assist you in getting on it that will help you along. Why? Because it's part of our divine purpose. We will go more in depth about divine purpose in Section II of this book. If you make a mistake or a different choice and the outcome isn't what you wanted, your guides will never say, "I told you so." They will lovingly support you and assist you back into the direction you need to go without doing it for you; and when you ask for assistance.

This makes another important point about Free Will. Your guides, angels, ascended masters will only assist you directly when asked. If you don't ask, they will not step in. If you want healing, you must ask. If you want direction and guidance on life issues, you must ask. If you need spiritual protection from negative energy on earth, you must ask. Asking may come in the form of meditation, prayer, decreeing, affirmations, or just plain inner talking. That being said, they were also there before you were born helping you plan your divine blueprint, so when they nudge and guide, it's still according to your what you put in your life plan for this life. So, those nudges and redirects can be about keeping you on track.

To give you an example of asking for guidance on whether you should do something or not: A few years ago, I had an opportunity to sell my essential oils and various other holistic products at a holiday gift show. I kept receiving guidance that I shouldn't do it. That it was not going to work out. I ignored it, and in the end their guidance was spot on. There was very little foot traffic and by the end of the night, I sold only two items, and this was after a lot of time and effort planning and setting up. I kept doing these types of shows and kept getting the same results. One time though, I received intuitive guidance to pull out my huge bag of hand-crocheted scarves to display with my holistic supplies. And wouldn't you know it, it was those scarves that were my big seller and I made a few hundred dollars during that particular holiday boutique. This was the only time I made any money at one of these types of shows. Clearly it wasn't in my life plan to do boutique and holiday fairs. Needless to say though, I learned to listen to my inner guidance, and I can also say the quality of my life is much better when I listen to my guides even if it seems unusual, weird, and/or out of my comfort zone. When you succeed in learning a life lesson, achieving or overcoming a challenge or fear, the elation and joy you feel afterwards is tremendous. Your perception about the very thing you resisted changes so radically that it moves you forward in your thinking, and you feel ready for new challenges, new opportunities to stretch your emotional flexibility and broaden your experiences.

I leave you with one more example as it relates to new challenges that stretch your emotional flexibility: Growing up through my teens, twenties, thirties and even early forties, it was my belief that I was incapable of being a leader of anything. I believed myself to be the force behind the leader because I was organized, conscientious and extremely helpful and competent. As I began my own spiritual journey around the age of 41, and began working on myself. Opportunities to realize that growth came forward. Three years ago, I was asked if I would step in and become co-president of my children's elementary school's PTA (Parent Teacher Association). Me, co-president? I reminded myself that I was not a natural-born leader, yet I not only accepted this huge challenge, I accepted a second term as well. Talk about stretching my emotional flexibility; I learned so much that it would take another book to explain what I achieved and gained from the experience. All of which continues to benefit me to this day. Things that I had to do that were scary are not so scary anymore. I learned a lot about myself and my perception of me changed dramatically. That's not to say I didn't make mistakes during those two years, but I didn't let little mistakes bring me down or allow me to give up. I learned from every one of them and it moved me forward. I know I was successful because I called for spiritual support and help ALL the time. Without my guides, spiritual teachers and God support, I would not have achieved what I did during those two years.

One more point I'd like to add to this story. This guidance to become PTA president came in the form of my husband. When I asked him if I should accept the position, he surprised me by saying yes. Him saying yes to a very demanding outside commitment was extremely unusual for him, so it made me pay attention. So much so, that I listened to the spiritual guidance that came through my spouse and accepted this leadership position. This is just another way that Spirit can communicate with you. Interesting huh?

Utilizing Free Will is the best way to keep connected to God, to your source of inner guidance, because it's about you constantly making the choice to let them assist you in all aspects of your day-to-day life. As your life unfolds through school, college, and your twenties, training yourself to develop intuitively, spiritually and divinely will put you on the path to all the life attributes we aspire to, like happiness, prosperity and inner peace. I conclude this chapter with one last quote, taken from *The Magic Presence*, by Godfre Ray King.

"The personal self of every individual is endowed with the Power of Choice (*free will*) as to what it wishes to think, to feel, to create and experience. If one uses all the substance and energy of his Being constructively, then Peace, Expansion, Joy, Opulence, and Glory are the return unto Life for the

Outpouring of Its Gifts. If one chooses and creates otherwise, his misery and destruction return into himself and destroy his body." [*The Magic Presence, King, Godfre Ray, Saint Germain Press. Pg. 95*]

Chapter 4

Our Energy Systems and Bodies

Our bodies are magnificently designed and when we learn how to use all the features built into them, we realize just how lucky we are in how we were built. This human body of ours has more than just the physical aspect of our body. It has energy centers and invisible bodies that store every teeny, tiny bit of information that has ever been said, done, thought or felt in all of our lifetimes since our soul came into existence. Our energy centers are constantly spinning, and working to connect our physical bodies to our invisible bodies – making sure that when we want to, we can always have a connection to God, and our guides and angels.

Let's talk about energy. Every single human, animal, plant is made up of energy. Every object, from the cars we drive to the homes we live in to the furniture we sit on and sleep in, is made up of energy. What makes everything seem solid to our eyes is the density of an object or person and the speed which the energy's frequency is on. But, think about it, if you put a piece of wood, a piece of steel, cells from the body, from a plant, under a special microscope, what do you see? The cells and atoms are moving. Energy also leaves a signature, a memory of having been there. It's in the air. It lingers on our furniture, our clothing, and of course our physical beings and invisible energy fields if we let it. It is up to us to clear what we don't want or what doesn't belong there. More about clearing and protecting ourselves later in the book.

Our Four Lower Bodies

First, I want to introduce you to all of your bodies. You've already met your physical body, which you know quite well. I will just add one thing – your human body is not who you are.

It's the outer garment you wear as a human in this lifetime. You aren't your body; you *have* a body. So I'm going to focus my discussion on the invisible bodies.

The Etheric Body – Is an exact duplicate of our physical body, but in energy form. It is the first energetic field that surrounds our physical body. The energetic radiance of this body is what we call our aura. Because this body is superimposed over our physical body, when we suffer illness, disease, loss of a limb or an internal organ on our physical body, it is still visible in our etheric body. There is an advanced technology called Kirlian photography used by scientists that shows a visual "memory" of the missing body part even though it's physically been removed from the person. The etheric body carries the energetic map or blueprint of our bodies and has the ability to generate new cells for healing and growth. The physical body is so energetically connected and dependent on the etheric body for cellular guidance that the physical body cannot exist without the etheric body. There are many energy and intuitive healers and practitioners who can see auras, and can detect illness or imbalances before they reach the physical body. The etheric body carries a higher frequency than the physical, and interestingly is the body that travels when we sleep, dream and/or do spiritual work.

The Astral Body – Often called the emotional body, this is considered to be the seat of our emotions. As with the etheric body, the astral body is also superimposed over the physical body. It's very fluid in its appearance and is one of the larger energy fields surrounding our body. The frequency of this body is much higher than that of the physical and etheric bodies, and is only visible through the gifted eye of a clairvoyant. Think of water, and of water being a great conductor. Our astral/emotional body is a energetic conductor to our emotions. Emotions are recorded through our astral body, and stored in our etheric body as well as the cells of our physical body. Every emotion you have ever experienced from this life, as well as past lives, and also from yourself as well as from others is stored there. That's why many holistic or spiritual healing methods are ideal for removing the negative or harmful emotions for balanced mental and psychological health. If we are healthy emotionally, then naturally our physical body is healthy.

The Mental Body – This body extends beyond the range of the astral body, and resonates at a frequency still higher than the previous three bodies. While the astral body is comprised of energies derived from our emotions, the mental body energies come from our thoughts and concrete intellect. Our thoughts through the mental body will have an active effect on our astral body. This gives the charge that converts our thoughts into actions which can have either a positive effect or a negative effect depending on what is being generated through our thoughts and emotions. In addition to negatively affecting our body if your thoughts are depressing, angry, bitter, jealous, etc., you will attract external energies that have the same frequency and momentum as your negative/ emotional thought process. The mental body communicates with the astral/emotional body which causes reactions to the etheric and ultimately our physical body depending on what information is being fed into it. The mental body is also a vehicle through which our creativity manifests. This body is also connected to the spiritual realm of the Divine Wisdom of God making the physical brain a means to project thoughts on the physical plane.

The energy fields of the above four, lower bodies extend beyond approximately three feet around our physical body – usually beyond our reach when our arms are outstretched.

Our Higher Bodies

The Causal Body – The causal body, through the personality's journey in physical experience, becomes an ever-expanding Sun and a Self-sustaining, Outpouring of Limitless ideas, Love, Wisdom and Power, flowing out forever on Rays of Love to the rest of this Universe. [*The Magic Presence, King, Godfre Ray, Saint Germain Press. Pg. 96*] All positive constructive actions, and experiences had through your various lifetimes are also stored in the Causal Body. Another name for the Causal Body would be the "Higher Self."

The Electronic Body – This perfect, Eternal, Electronic Body exists from twelve to fifty feet above the physical body of every individual, unless one is a very low or destructive type, when It withdraws still farther away…the Electronic Body of every Individualized Flame of God is a Dazzling, Blazing Light of such intensity that the human eyes can only gaze upon It for a fraction of a second. …To It, the personal self should look for the Supply of every good thing as a child looks to its mother. All that is within the God Flame flows into the Electronic Body, where the Tremendous Power and Intensity of the Light of the 'Mighty I AM Presence' is stepped down to a degree that can act in the vibratory octave of the physical world. [*The Magic Presence, King, Godfre Ray, Saint Germain Press. Pg. 99*]

The Chakras

The human body has seven energy centers that circle around the body. Chakra is the Sanskrit word for "wheel." Each wheel spins and whirls around the body in a clockwise fashion. Each of these seven energy centers are located at different points of our body and connected to locations of our body from the base of the spine to the top of the head. Each chakra corresponds to an area of life we must master in order to clear our karma, heal and purify in order to ascend towards God. Each chakra has a corresponding color, and connects with specific organs within an area of the body. When a chakra is out of alignment, the color and direction of the chakra can be off, and out of balance. If one chakra is too strong, its color can dominate the next chakra. For a clairvoyant healer, that would be an indicator of some imbalances both on the physical as well as the mental/emotional planes. I'd also like to briefly mention there are five other chakras including one below our feet, one between our heart and throat chakra and the other three above the seventh chakra. For the purposes of this book, we will focus on the seven main chakras.

1st Chakra – Root Chakra (Location: Base of the Spine)
Color: Red
Organs connected to this chakra are: legs, feet, base of spine, immune system, rectum
Emotional/Mental Traits:

- Connected with basic survival instincts
- Primal feelings of fear
- Feelings of grounded-ness and connection to the earth
- Family culture and values
- Standing up for yourself
- Ability to support yourself

Illnesses connected to imbalances in the root chakra:

- Sciatica
- Lower back problems
- Rectal cancer
- Hemorrhoids
- Immune-related diseases

2nd Chakra – Sacral Chakra (Location: lower abdomen-navel area)
Color: Orange (Also known as "seat of our intuition and creativity")

Organs connected to this chakra are: bladder, sex organs, pelvis, spleen, lower intestines, hip region, appendix

Emotional/Mental Traits:

- Connects to emotional and sexual energy
- Ability to procreate
- Creative center
- Deals with partnerships of all kinds: romantic, business, professional
- Finances
- Power and control

Illnesses connected to imbalances in sacral chakra:

- Colitis
- Lower back pain
- Sciatic
- Urinary/bladder problems
- Constipation (also connects with root chakra)
- Reproductive problems
- Pelvic/hip problems

3rd Chakra – Solar Plexus Chakra (Location: below sternum to navel)

Color: Yellow

Organs connected to this chakra are: stomach, liver, pancreas, kidneys, adrenals, gall bladder, small intestines, mid-spine

Emotional/Mental Traits:

- Area of personal power
- Anger issues
- Self-esteem/self-confidence/self-worth
- Aggression or victim/cowardly
- Trust/security
- Fear
- Care of oneself and others
- Worry

Illnesses connected to imbalances in the solar plexus chakra:

- Stomach/gastric problems like ulcers
- Liver problems
- Diabetes
- Arthritis
- Anorexia/bulimia
- Adrenal problems
- Indigestion/reflux

4th Chakra – Heart Chakra (Location: center of chest)

Color: Green

Organs connected to this chakra are: heart, lungs, thymus, ribs, upper spine, diaphragm, circulatory system, arms, shoulders

Emotional/Mental Traits:

- Love/unconditional love/self-love
- Grief
- Loneliness
- Commitment
- Forgiveness
- Compassion and empathy
- Self-centeredness
- Hate
- Depression

Illnesses connected to imbalances in the heart chakra:

- Heart problems
- Lung problems
- Bronchial pneumonia
- Asthma
- Autoimmune diseases – i.e., lupus, rheumatoid arthritis
- Upper spine
- Allergies
- Lung cancer
- AIDS/HIV

5th Chakra – Throat Chakra (Location: Throat)

Color: Blue

Organs connected to throat chakra are: throat, thyroid, parathyroid, sinuses, mouth teeth, gums, jaw, trachea, esophagus, neck

Emotional/Mental Traits:

- All issues relating to communication
- Verbal expression
- Will to communicate your truth
- Ability/inability to express creativity
- Issues of criticism, judgment, anger
- Expression of needs, desires, dreams

Illnesses connected to imbalances in the throat chakra:

- Chronic sore throats
- Laryngitis
- All thyroid problems
- Scoliosis
- TMJ (jaw clicking/pain)
- Gum inflammation and canker sores
- Teeth issues
- Swollen glands
- Metabolic disorders
- Throat or thyroid cancer

6th Chakra – Third Eye or Brow Chakra (Location: Center of forehead)

Color: Violet

Organs connected to the 6th chakra are: eyes, pituitary gland, nervous system, brain, spinal cord, nose, ears, sinuses

Emotional/Mental Traits:

- Self-evaluation
- Truth
- Intellect
- Expansiveness/openness to new ideas

- Flexibility of mind others ideas
- Emotional intelligence

Illnesses connected to the brow chakra:

- Endocrine/glandular imbalances
- Seizures
- Cataracts and other eye problems
- Glaucoma
- Blindness
- Learning disabilities
- Brain tumors
- Neurological problems/diseases
- Spinal issues
- Sinus conditions
- Ear infections
- Deafness

7th Chakra – Crown Chakra (Location: Top of Head)

Color: Purple

Organs associated with the crown chakra are: cerebral cortex, general nervous system functioning, pineal gland, muscular systems, skeletal systems and skin

Emotional/Mental Traits:

- Devotion/spirituality
- Prophetic thoughts
- Transcendent thoughts/ideas
- Faith
- Receptive to divine healing guidance
- Selfless service
- Values and ethics

Illnesses connected to the crown chakra:

- Alzheimer's disease or dementia
- Psychosis
- Bipolar disorder
- Schizophrenia

- Energy disorders
- Extreme sensitivity to light
- Various mental disorders

The seven chakras are divided into lower and upper. The four lower chakras relate to the earth and the four elements, earth (root chakra), water (sacral chakra), fire (solar plexus) and air (heart) with the heart center being the transitional chakra connecting the lower more earthly chakras with the upper connecting to the higher spiritual energies through the throat, brow and crown chakras. On the path to ascension, all chakras must be cleared of karma and purified to function perfectly as they were meant to be.

Exercise:
An excellent meditation/visualization for you to try out. Prepare yourself by sitting in a comfortable chair (or you can do this at bedtime while lying down) and begin to visualize each chakra. Notice the color and energetic movement. Visualize breathing into that chakra. Focus your breath there, beginning with the root chakra. Whether you sense or see that it is imbalanced, visualize that chakra as clear and spinning perfectly clockwise. If it is imbalanced, correct/heal the imbalance, visualize the correct color and movement and stay a moment or two longer to restore it. Then move up to the next chakra and do the same. Visualize, balance and breathe into each chakra through to the crown chakra. When you've completed your scan, take a deep breath, hold it for ten seconds or so allowing the breath to penetrate all of your chakras and blow out hard cleansing them of all stress, strain and negativity. You will feel lighter and more relaxed when you are done.

If you have a time constraint but still want to do this, visualize/scan all seven at once, spinning clockwise. Then do the deep breath for 10 seconds to cleanse out stress and negativity three times. This you can do in the car (as long as someone else is driving), on your way to a playing in a sport, performing in a concert or other performance activity or even before a social event.

Chapter 5

Archangels:
Who They Are and How They Serve

Throughout childhood you may have felt drawn or connected to one or more of the Archangels. If you were, you have been very blessed indeed. They are pure, unconditionally loving light beings whose purpose is to serve God through serving humanity. If you've connected to them, how lucky were you to experience the feeling of tremendous unconditional loving support, peace and healing. If you haven't work with the Archangels, here's a little tutorial on who they are and how to connect with them.

Now, the Archangels are in what we would call leadership roles working over a particular area of service. There is a hierarchy of Archangels, with legions of angels serving under the Archangels' leadership within these particular service areas. For instance, there are healing angels, protecting angels, angels of love and harmony, angels of peace, angels for purification, etc.

This book will focus on the seven primary Archangels serving in seven key areas of life. Briefly these seven qualities are: power, wisdom, love, purity, healing, peace, freedom.

Let's begin:

Archangel Michael is the Archangel of Power, Protection and Faith. He serves under the first ray of Power and the Will of God. The color of the ray he serves under is blue. In religious and spiritual texts, he figures prominently as one of the highest Archangels serving in the Angelic realm. He is recognized in Christian, Jewish and Islamic faiths as the greatest and most revered of all the Archangels. In religious paintings and artwork he is often depicted holding his blue sword unsheathed vanquishing or ready to vanquish evil beings or entities.

Archangel Michael is a very special angel to us. He, with his legions of light, has dedicated himself for thousands and thousands of years to the safety, the security, the perfectionment of our souls and to our protection; caring for us, sponsoring us, rebuking us, teaching us the way of God's Holy will, giving us to understand that we each have a blueprint in life, that we have a divine plan. [*The Masters and Their Retreats, Prophet, Mark L and Elizabeth, Pg. 232*]

Call to beloved Archangel Michael when you need protection, when you need to bolster your faith in yourself, your path, or your divinity. Call to Michael when you need support in leadership roles in your life, in protecting and securing your personal power. Archangel Michael says, "You may call on me daily for protection and for securing your sense of personal power. All those who call on me will receive my assistance instantaneously. I encourage you to call on me daily if you are so drawn."

Archangel Jophiel is the Archangel of Wisdom, Understanding, and Knowledge. He serves under the second ray of Wisdom and Illumination and serves with World Teachers, Jesus and Kuthumi. Jophiel means "Beauty of God." The color of the ray he serves under is a golden yellow, and the radiations emanate through our crown chakra. They assist with the illumination of mankind in recognizing through knowledge and understanding of their 'Mighty I AM Presence,' encouraging the opening of their minds to expand and learn all there is to know of earth and spirit. Beloved Jophiel and his Twin Flame assist those who choose the path of teaching, counseling, education, nursing, and many matters of the intellect as understood through our pure God-Selves. They also assist and tend to our living Mother Earth and all of the elementals, water, air, earth and fire.

Archangel Jophiel says, "Beloved readers, I am here to support you on your path in ways of knowledge, illumination, in helping you to realize your place in the universe, to develop an understanding of it through intuitive knowledge and wisdom. Should your path be connected to the second ray, I can be of service when you call on me."

Archangel Chamuel is the Archangel of Divine Love and Beauty. He serves on the third ray of Love, Creativity and Beauty. The color of this ray is pink. Chamuel means "He who seeks God." Chamuel's Twin Flame is named Charity. Together with their legions of pink-flame angels, Chamuel and Charity serve to expand the flame of adoration and divine love within the hearts of men and elementals. Chamuel and Charity are devoted to the children of earth, in preventing evil and fallen spirits from harming or magnetizing negative, energetic forces that would keep children of all ages from God, divine love and support. They will support and assist you in all areas of love and harmony, including family relationships, friendships, and love for humanity.

Under the third ray, Chamuel will also assist in pursuits of creativity in music, art, sculpture, or in other areas where creativity would serve such as school or committee projects and programs, fundraising activities, social and school events, and similar pursuits where being creative is beneficial for an ideal outcome for the good of all.

Unconditional love conquers all and everyone. If the foundation of your being and emotional state is truly reflecting a powerful feeling of unconditional love, you would be amazed at how much you can transform a situation or another individual's perception and feelings. I've seen it myself over and over again. Love truly conquers all. The key to this is being genuine and not just your words, or surface expression. When we emanate love from within as if we are glowing with this divine love, nothing can harm us of the external, but we as "love/light beings" can transform others.

> Archangel Chamuel says, "Call on me for all issues of love. If you need love, call on me, if you need love in a difficult situation, call on me. Call on me to soothe an angry teacher, parent, friend, a stranger and even yourself. We answer your every call, but you must first call."

Archangel Gabriel is the Archangel of Purity, Hope and Joy. He serves on the fourth ray of Purity, Discipline and Joy. This is also the ray of Ascension and the color of this ray is white. As a mother myself, Gabriel has a special place in my heart as he helps both the mother and her unborn child during pregnancy.

> Gabriel salutes each mother-to-be with the glad tidings of the coming of the Christ for whom she is privileged to prepare the body temple. He places the electronic pattern of the Christ Self of the incoming child within the aura of the mother in order that the body elementals of mother and child, under the direction of their Christ selves, may work together to bring forth the perfect form. The angelic hosts work with the parents to anchor in the child the highest and best talents developed in previous embodiments and stored in the causal body. [*The Masters and Their Retreats, Prophet, Mark L. and Elizabeth, Pg. 53-54*]

Beloved Archangel Gabriel is also a champion of children, and is very supportive and helpful to sensitive and gifted children, teens and young adults. Gabriel is often associated with the water element as he too can be a soother of the emotions. Gabriel's Twin flame is Hope. Hope fills the parents with expectancy, joy, enthusiasm and the memory of the goal of every life stream: the ascension in the light. [*The Masters*

37

and Their Retreats, Prophet, Mark L. and Elizabeth, Pg. 54] Gabriel is often in the role of messenger, as he was the beloved Archangel who spoke to Mary to let her know she was chosen by God and was with child, our Beloved Jesus.

Archangel Gabriel says, "White. I encourage you to wear white as white is reflective of the light within yourself, of the purity of your higher self and electronic body. White carries all of the colors, and so wearing too much black or wearing black too often will draw to you what you least want; which is negative energies from other people, lower energies from the astral plane and in general the very negative energy that is collected about the planet from greed, anger, jealousy, hardness and meanness. Wearing black clothing draws in energy, while wearing white reflects energy. Bring out your light because your inner light heals all who come in contact with you – either through deliberate contact as in your relationships and friendships as well as random contact as in passing by strangers during your day. All who journey towards to the Path to God, journey in the Light. Go forth, call in your 'Mighty I AM Presence' and be that Light."

Archangel Raphael is the Archangel of Healing. He serves on the fifth ray of Healing, Divine Truth, Concrete Science and Abundance. The color of this ray is green. The name Raphael means "God cures" in Hebrew. Because this ray corresponds to the Third Eye chakra (center of forehead), it is also the ray of intuitive vision. By being able to open our third eye, we are able to see and understand many, many things such as how to heal ourselves, how to draw enough supply and abundance, how to create and manifest what we want within ourselves and our world.

Traditionally, Raphael has always been associated with healing, but he is also able to assist us in opening up our inner vision to find our truth and to understand our purpose. Those who have an affinity for healing, as a future profession in all the many types of healing from traditional medical fields, like nursing and medicine, to alternative healing in the many holistic, and natural healing modalities, including energy and intuitive healing, as well as those who are musicians, mathematics or wish to be scientists – may likely be serving on the fifth ray.

Call on Archangel Raphael for healing – of all health, emotional and mental issues. Archangel Raphael says, "Healing is about the journey to God. When we heal all of our illnesses, we also end up healing our relationships, our life lessons – and ultimately our perceptions of all these things which brings us to a new perception, that of which is through our God-Self which, of course, is our most unconditionally loving and compassionate self. When that is healed, the capacity for joy, peace, harmony, abundance and greater love will be your legacy. I am here along with Mother Mary to assist you in any way you wish. Just call upon me for healing and support."

Archangel Uriel is the Archangel of Peace and Divine Service. He serves on the sixth ray of Peace, Service and Brotherhood. The color of this ray is purple and gold. In Hebrew, Uriel means "Light of God." Uriel teaches us devotion to God, and service to humanity as being the most important contribution we can make. Uriel says, "For when we are selfless in our divine service and devoted to peace and love, we draw more light into ourselves which thus raises our vibration and casts out negativity on all levels. This will go a long way to helping us purify our bodies. When divine love, light and peace are residing within us because we are taking great joy in our service to others, how can the evils and greed of the world find room in such a pure body. The answer is, it can't. There's no room for it, and so it must dissolve, or disappear into the universe."

Joy is the key to selfless service. It's not pure intent and service if we feel put upon, taken advantage of, or unhappy to be doing something for someone else. That doesn't mean you need to feel great joy in doing the dishes, household chores, or other similar boring and tedious chores. Acceptance that this must done, and satisfaction from doing it well is plenty when it comes to this type of service activity. But, complaining because you made a commitment to help your friend move house, or do a school project, or shoveling snow for your neighbor is not going to bring you closer to God. It will, in fact, create a barrier to God. A barrier or feeling of aloneness that you will have created with the negative emotions you created because you are unhappy doing these things. On your pathway way to joy, you must be willing to surrender and accept. When you have conquered surrender and acceptance, you will find peace. There will be a whole host of other wonderful emotions such as excitement, anticipation, harmony, camaraderie, connectedness, and of course love and compassion. You will find when you approach any kind of service with a positive attitude, you will attract that which you glow with.

Beloved Archangel Uriel is especially a champion of children, teens and adults through age 33. He is particularly concerned with the emotional and spiritual well-being of this age group because there is so much war, violence, fear, anger and indifference. These negative expressions are hurting your beautiful and loving energies which are inherent in you.

Archangel Uriel gives us an exercise for letting go of fear. He says to place your hands, one over the other, to your heart, then release them, opened, relaxed, extending them outwards. Uncross your legs and breathe gently. Then speak these words tenderly to your soul and to your body three times: "Peace, be still!" When you hold your hands out in front of you, cupped, the posture reflects the serenity of the little child within you, secure in the arms of its mother. [*The Masters and Their Retreats, Prophet, Mark L. and Elizabeth, Pg. 299*]

Archangel Uriel is the Angel of the Resurrection Flame. This Flame brings about rejuvenation, renewal and rebirth to us as we become reborn into our true God-Selves. Call to Beloved Uriel for assistance in your service, for helping you establish peace and inner harmony in times of stress and conflict. As with all our loving Archangels, they come instantly when we call to them.

Archangel Zadkiel is the Archangel of Freedom and Transformation. He serves on the seventh ray of Freedom, Justice and Forgiveness. The color of this ray is violet. The name Zadkiel means "Righteousness of God." Freedom in this context means the freeing of ourselves from the bindings of our negativity, of our restricted thinking, and limited perspective of our surrounding world. Once we break those bindings that have been created by our ego within our current embodiment, and merge with our 'I AM Presence,' we feel the release into freedom and transformation.

Through him as well as the Lord of the Seventh Ray, we receive the gift of the Violet Flame. This healing gift when called upon by us helps to heal us on many levels including past-life karma, issues for our current life, physical health programs that are drawn from negative emotional patterns that hold us back to fulfill present life in ways that are joyous, abundant and divinely loving.

Zadkiel and Holy Amethyst (his Twin Flame) are here for one purpose; to help us secure our individual freedom so that when we are set free, we can free our households, our towns, our nations, our planet. The main block to our freedom is our negative karma. We can transmute it with the violet-flame decrees. We can also balance negative karma by sending forth divine love and compassionately-human love and calling upon the law of mercy and forgiveness. Saint Germain tells us the joy is the motor of life, and the violet flame is the fuel. Forgiveness and mercy are qualities of this flame. [*The Masters and Their Retreats, Prophet, Mark L. and Elizabeth, Pg. 388*]

Zadkiel says, "The key to freedom is forgiveness, forgiveness for others, for situations that you felt were beyond your control when they went badly, and most importantly forgiveness of yourself. In forgiving yourself, you will have the realization that the only person you can change is you. When you heal and transform yourself, your relationships and outlook on external life will reflect brightness and light. You will gain a perspective of compassion for your fellow human beings in a way you never felt before because you will no longer carry the emotional burdens of pain, anger, sadness and all other negative emotions."

Exercise:
Here's a wonderful way to practice working with the Archangels. They all vibrate at different frequencies, and their energies will have a different sensation that helps you identify them once you begin working with them regularly. During some quiet time in your bedroom, or alone time when you will not be disturbed, close your eyes, relax and focus your breathing. (It's always best to sit on a chair, back straight, feet planted on the floor, legs and arms uncrossed. Hands on lap resting open.)

Slowly, begin calling Archangel Michael. Say his name slowly three times. Then tune in and begin to feel his energy. Give yourself one to two minutes of sensing him. You will notice that if you are in a calm quiet state, you can easily and quickly feel his presence. Acknowledge him, let him know that you plan on calling upon him more often to assist you and thank him for transmitting his energy through you this day and sense him leave before you move on. Continue your meditation with Archangels, Jophiel, Chamuel, Gabriel, Raphael, Uriel and Zadkiel. You will notice that each of their energies vibrate differently. You may even sense them in different areas of your body. Use the same format for calling them in each time. And always thank them for their assistance. By doing all seven in this particular meditation exercise, you will begin to become familiar with their energies. Once that is learned, you will know and recognize immediately how quickly they come upon your call.

Chapter 6

Guardian Angels and Spirit Guides: Your Spiritual Support System

We have an amazing spiritual support system that is meant just for us during our lifetime on earth. In the previous chapter you have learned about the loving support of the seven Archangels serving on the Seven Rays of God. This chapter will focus on your own personal spiritual support system. These beloved beings are here specifically to assist and support *you* during your entire life. While some may be with you for a specified amount of time, others will remain with you throughout your entire life. Every human being that is born has the same spiritual support system in place. A support system that was planned and determined before you were born in order to help you conquer life lessons, discover your talents and gifts and more…in order to fulfill your divine purpose and soul contract.

As you can see as you read through each chapter, you are not alone. You have never been all alone. There have always been loving spirits and beings by your side even though you might have been unaware, or have felt isolated and cut off from this loving support.

Spirit Guides

Every human being whether they are spiritual or atheists, has spirit guides assisting, protecting, and teaching them. Over the years I have read many books about spirit guides, as well as having my own personal experience with my guides through meditation and journey work. Here is what I have learned.

Everyone has what is called a "master guide" who is with you for all of your life. They were assigned to you before birth to be your guide through this particular lifetime. Just to be clear, this is not your guardian angel. (Your guardian angel is a separate being of which will be discussed in the second half of this chapter.) All of your guides have tremendous unconditional love for you. There's nothing you can say or do that would prevent them from loving you in this way. One of their main purposes is to keep you on your divine path with the hope that you will follow through with your divine purpose as you planned before you came into this lifetime. They help in a great many other ways as well if you let them. As with all spiritual beings, they must follow the law of free will. They can suggest, and guide, but ultimately it's your choice.

Whether you were aware of them before reading this book or not, you would do very well to begin a relationship with them daily or regularly. Your master guide can be male or female. They can be individuals from past lives. They can be wise spiritual teachers from any ancient time. An ancient Greek healer, a Native American Indian chief, an Egyptian scholar, as well as someone that has a modern, everyday appearance with a common name like John or Marie. For example, my master guide is a wonderful female being who looks like she had a lifetime during the 1950s. Her dress and appearance are representative of that lifetime, and her name I had come to learn is Ella.

In addition to your master guide who remains with you all of your life, you will have any number of additional spirit guides supporting you in various capacities and at various times depending on what you are doing in that period of your life – whether it be working out karmic relationships, talents and abilities, or teaching you skills that will put you on your professional path. You can have many spirit guides. It is not limited to any particular number. I've felt anywhere from five to seven guides at different times in my life. I've included a guided meditation in the appendix that you can record with your voice and use to assist you in meeting your spirit guides and initiate a more visual or intuitive relationship with them.

Now spirit guides exist in the spiritual realm in the octave immediately below the ascended masters. Serving in the capacity of spirit guide is part of their service to humanity, and assists them in their personal growth within the spiritual realm. Even though they serve at a level lower than the Beloved Ascended Masters, they serve at a very high level indeed. If they didn't possess a certain level of purity and attain a high level of unconditional love then they wouldn't be qualified to serve as spirit guides. This is important as you never want to engage with anyone lower than our spirit guides, angels or ascended masters for those that exist in the astral plane have not cleared their karma and negativity, and could confuse, misdirect or harm you on your path. When meditating or simply calling for spiritual guidance or support, you must always ask for spirit guides, or spirit beings from the *highest level*. You do not want to attract spirits or entities in the astral plane. This is where earthbound spirits exist who have not been to the "Light," as well as other negative entities who do not have your best interests at heart. They may be entities that carry fear, jealousy, anger and other harmful emotions that could misdirect and influence you in a bad way. Although I will be discussing several ways to protect yourself, simply calling in a circle of white light to encompass you before you meditate or engage in intuitive dialogue with your spirit guides or angels, will provide the necessary protection to you. But, still you must also request guidance from the highest-level guides to ensure no lower entities feel allowed or welcomed to come in. You can also simply ask Archangel Michael for protection while you are meditating.

Spirit guides serve in many wonderful and helpful ways. You may call upon them for everyday things like help with finding a parking space, a good seat in class, sporting event, or concert. They would be helpful in locating things you have misplaced, or need to find when you are shopping, etc. Always be respectful and grateful when calling upon them for assistance. There are spirit guides that can help out at a given moment when needed. If you are stumped on a problem, need assistance in working out a relationship, or help with a solution to anything, call on them and they will be most helpful. Some guides are enlisted as "teachers." They are here to teach you during a particular life lesson, or period in your life where you need to learn something from a situation, or learn *how to* do something. You may have different spirit teachers throughout your life depending on what you need to learn, or even what you are doing professionally. There are also spirit guides that help with healing, and can come to your aid for all types of healing. They may also let you know when you need to pay attention to your health in the same manner as our spirit-guide team.

The key here in working with your spirit guides who assist in all forms is being open to their suggestions and assistance. We have, at all times, the choice of taking their advice or not. This again is because of Free Will. They cannot force you to do something you do not wish to do, but I can tell you from personal experience, they usually offer the best course of action, soundest advice, and most suitable solutions to our problems, because they can see from a perspective that we cannot.

How to tell the difference between guidance from your spirit guide and interference from other lower level entities is very simple. Your spirit guides will usually provide information that is always loving and helpful. You will never get an "icky" feeling in your body, or feelings of insecurity, low self-esteem, anger, or sadness. Often when you receive guidance through you mind, it may feel like your own thoughts, but when you examine the information, you will often realize this would not be something you would have ever thought of on your own. A great example is the writing of this book. This suggestion would not have been an original idea from me. I have had careers in magazine publishing in the area of advertising, and as a healer. Writing a book was most definitely out of my comfort zone. I could have said to myself, "Oh, this will be too hard.Will I be able to write in a clear manner that my readers will find interesting. Do I know enough about the subject to elaborate on any one topic in the book." Instead, I evaluated, meditated and asked for validation that this was the right path...then slowly began the process. I can tell you that following this guidance is already starting to pay off. It feels right when I go to my computer each day. I look forward to writing. I try to never miss a day of writing, even if it's only long enough to write two sentences. The fact that you are reading this book tells me that I was right to follow my guidance.

This brings up another important point. If you have gone through the trouble of learning how to work with your guides, feel the beginnings of confidence in what you receive in your guidance, then when you hear or receive something that seems a little out of your usual thought process, pay attention. This could be really, really, really good for you in a way that will expand you, elevate your character, talent or skill levels in order to advance you to something you never knew you wanted until you were ready for it. There are many, many experiences I have had over my whole life because even as a teenager, I was open to new experiences.

I'll give you another example in the form of a lovingly remembered memory. When I was in elementary school, I was painfully shy. I couldn't imagine speaking in front of an audience. In my ten-year-old mind, that was just not even a consideration. Then, I must have received very strong guidance from my spirit guides (even before I knew that I had them, let alone who they were), because something very unusual for me happened. I was nearing the end of my sixth grade, about a month before graduation. The teacher invited any student to step up if they were interested in giving a speech at their graduation. My first thought was – definitely NOT ME. That night though, I laid in bed sleepless and thought about what I would say in a speech. I practically wrote the entire speech in my mind. When I was done mentally writing the speech, the next day I actually wrote it and handed it in to my teacher scared out of my wits at the thought of what I was about to do. Shy, quiet and mousy me had decided to write an original speech that I would read out loud to my classmates, parents and teachers. Well, I did it, and I can't tell you how excited I was at being able to do this successfully. Looking back at that moment now, I know that this set the stage for many other occasions where I would stand up in front of different types of audiences speaking for many different reasons. That was one of the most pivotal moments of my life. I didn't know it then, but I've come to realize that if I hadn't made that scary leap, hadn't done this, the entire course of my life would have been very, very different than it is now. I could fill another whole book of the opportunities, and experiences that followed through to today that would *not* have happened if I hadn't written and read my speech at my sixth-grade graduation.

The lesson here is to not discount any guidance that seems out of the ordinary. Unless you know without a doubt that this would be harmful to you or to another person, there's no reason not to try. There's a difference between my guides telling me to do a speech, from them telling me to doing something that is destructive. You will know the difference by the feelings in your body. You can be nervous about taking the leap, like making speeches, but don't let it paralyze you into not giving it a try. And, in doing this uncomfortable thing, you may still have failures, but that is its own lesson as to what you do with that failure. Failures teach us far more than successes. The story about my speech was pivotal because it set the tone for my entire life afterwards. Much of the time your intuitive guidance will help you run your life more easily, with more joy, and flow with positive solutions for all. *But*, there will be times that following your guidance will put you on a path that can have an effect that can change the course of your whole life…usually for the better. As a reader of this book if you are a teenager, college student or simply someone in their twenties, this kind of guidance could begin to happen at this time in your life. So pay attention, as it can set the tone for your entire life, as my speech did for me.

Guardian Angels

There are many definitions as to who or what guardian angels are. Are they a separate angel being? Are they our master spirit guide? Are they our Higher Selves? So many ideas and interpretations that it's hard to know what the truth is. Many of the teachings in these books contradict each other on the definition of a guardian angel. In my opinion, of these contrasting facts, is that for each person it was just a matter of perspective. We are all a sum total of our beliefs, what we've been taught and how we were raised, in combination with what we have experienced on a deeply personal level. Even at your relatively young age, you have already formed some beliefs based on experiences you may have had that gave you a very definite perspective that differs from your parents or friends. What I will add though, is the importance of learning to use your intuitive guidance in determining the spiritual level of any author whose books you will choose to read. (At the back of this book is an index of recommended reading to further your learning with trusted authors who are more spiritually or scientifically advanced than most.)

Anyone who has any kind of belief in God, a Higher Source, a Divine Power...also believes in guardian angels. It's comforting to know that there is a spiritual being that is strictly meant to be there just for you. I have read many, many, many books on spirit guides, and guardian angels over the years. Some of what I learned made perfect sense, and I applied what I learned successfully, but regarding "guardian angels," what resonated for me the most is what I learned from a series of books channeled by two pure human beings whose names are: Mr. and Mrs. Guy Ballard (pen names are Godfre Ray and Lotus King) through their publishing company, Saint Germain Press. These two individuals who are as pure of heart as any human can be, channeled the teachings of the Beloved Ascended Master, Saint Germain. When you read the teachings in these very special, green books, they speak to your heart in such a way that you know what you are learning is truth.

We are all taught that our guardian angel is with us throughout our lives. Our Electronic Body is just that. We are taught that they are there to protect us, love us unconditionally and are always there for us in an emergency or emotional crisis. Yes, yes and yes to all three in connection to how our 'I AM Presence' can function for us at any and all times. So, in other words your God-Self actually functions as your 'guardian angel.' How perfect is that. Your perfect and pure God-Self, who knows you better than any being on earth or in Heaven is your protector, healer and giver of unconditional love and support.

In Chapter 5, you learned about all of your bodies with the Electronic Body being your purest, most perfect part of you. Our God-Self, our 'Mighty I AM Presence' is the individualized being of God, connected to our God Source. We as human beings in our dense earth bodies are connected to our Electronic Body/God-Self making us one with God. If the Human Body was the God Source, each cell or organ of this body would be the individualized human being that is part of the whole body. A liver cannot function by itself. It needs to be part of the body to function and survive. That is the same as with our human and spiritual selves. Our Electronic Body provides the life force to our human body. Without it, we would die.

With that in mind, call and meditate with your guardian angel/Electronic Body as if it was a separate being, but remembering in your mind that it's so much more wonderful than that. It is your purest, most perfect self that contains everything – and I mean everything – you could ever need during your whole life. The better acquainted you are with your guardian angel, and the better you are able to connect with and tune in to your guardian angel, the better quality and more joyful and fulfilling life you will have.

Exercise:

Prepare as you would for any other meditation, making sure you will not be disturbed. Close your eyes, and take a few slow, deep breaths. Breathe in through the nose, and breathe out through the mouth. When breathing in, fill your abdomen with your intake of air. After you have calmed your mind and body, and released stress and negativity through your breath, call to your 'guardian angel' asking to feel his/her Presence in your heart region as your heart connects with the heart of your guardian angel. Take a moment with your eyes closed visualizing this happening while staying aware of the feelings in your body as you do this exercise. Begin to feel the energy of your God-Self/guardian angel surround you with soothing sensations around your body, mind and heart. Ask to feel her unconditional love for you. Thank him for always being there for you. You can also ask him to blend or overlight his energy over your body throughout the day. As you become in tune with the energy of your guardian angel, you will begin to recognize her anytime you meditate. Practice this brief meditation a few minutes immediately after you awaken in the morning.

Chapter 7

Karma and Reincarnation: Definition and Understanding

In preparing this chapter for you, I looked up in the dictionary of my Kindle for the definition of karma. Here is what it said:

Karma – the sum of a person's actions in this and previous states of existence, viewed as deciding their fate in future existences. <SPECIAL USAGE> informal, destiny or fate, following as effect from cause.

Did you find that definition helpful? I'm guessing not so much. Here's another one that may be easier to understand:

Karma – the universal law of balance, of cause and effect, where everything both good and bad must be repaid or balanced out.

That is a little clearer. Now, here's the definition of reincarnation:

Reincarnation – the rebirth of a soul in a new body.

This definition is short, sweet and to the point, but it lacks depth and understanding of the whys and hows of reincarnation. So, this chapter is completely devoted to understanding these two concepts and how they are interrelated.

What may have already become clear in this book if you've started with Chapter 1 is we are all born with a plan. We all carry burdens or challenges that we must overcome in the form of difficult relationships, traumatic life situations, obstacles on our paths, learning disabilities, emotional stuff, and so much more.

It's a matter of figuring out which are karma, and which are life lessons that you selected in order to have certain experiences which could increase or accelerate your spiritual progress.

Then, we get to try again, and again, and again, by being reborn over and over and over. On the one hand, it's comforting to know that living this one life on earth, isn't all there is. On the other hand, dying and starting all over again as an infant can seem scary or intimidating depending on how hard your life has been so far. So you wonder, just what *did* my soul plan for me that I am unaware of now that I am here? It planned plenty and this book will give you tools to unlock those secrets as you need to know them so they can guide you, comfort you and reassure you that everything that happens to you and around you is not by accident. There *is* a plan in place and by taking advantage and embracing all that's happening to you and around you, you will help in creating a better life for you on earth while at the same time advancing yourself spiritually to higher levels of under-standing, unconditional love, abundance, and inner peace. It's aaaalllll good, as they say.

So, let's back up a little to the very beginning; your beginning in this lifetime. Before your soul entered the body of the baby inside your mother's belly, even before she conceived you. Your guides and ascended master teachers helped you put together a soul plan, a blueprint of your life so to speak. This plan includes a great many things including how to heal your karma, work off karmic debt to others, and life lessons that would assist in helping you advance on your spiritual path. In Part II of this book, we will delve further into understanding divine purpose, and divine path, but in this section we are focusing on the meaning of karma and reincarnation to give you a foundation in which to understand why you are here.

Okay, so getting back to your beginnings. You are born on such and such date and year. You are this many years old right now. Looking back at your relatively short life thus far, consider how much you have accomplished, how easy or difficult your life has been. Consider your successes in the school, socially, family relationships, sports ability, musical or artistic talents. Consider your failures, obstacles to your progress or difficulties in your life thus far. Were you born with ADD or ADHD or other physical or mental handicap? Did you need occupational therapy so you could write and do other fine motor skills? Did or do you need extra academic support at school such as special education in math, English, science? Are you clumsy in gym or at sports? Do you stutter or have a speech impediment? Is it really hard to focus in class? Did you have trouble writing your letters and numbers because you were dyslexic? Did your parents get divorced, siblings get ill? Have you endured the loss of a loved one who died in an accident, or from a disease? Do you struggle socially, always feeling left out, awkward and lonely? Do you feel isolated all the time because you feel and think differently about things? Do you feel like no one "gets" you including maybe your parents or siblings? There are hundreds of situations that could be listed here. All of these situations can relate to your having to heal karma in this life based on how you behaved and treated people, situations *and* ourselves in our past lives. Also, the people you are born to, the people you meet through school, through friendships, work, in your neighborhood, are part of this process – even strangers can be part of the process. You are helping them heal, learn and grow as much as they are helping you heal, learn and grow. You are not together by accident but by amazing divine design.

If you feel you have a lot on your plate this lifetime around, it could be, because you wanted to accelerate your spiritual progress in order to achieve new levels of advancement. Do not despair. As you work with this book, and begin meditating and developing your intuition, you can handle any obstacle and challenge by staying focused on your path back to God. And as you work your way through this life, you will be able to find joy when you meditate and connect with your angels, guides and God-Self. It doesn't have to be a dreary existence even if you have a lot of karma to handle.

Now I can tell you thus far, without your realizing it, you've probably already dealt with many karmic relationships and issues. Check in with yourself, and think about a situation you felt that you handled well, or that you learned from through dealing with obstacles, or difficult people. Think about your successes in how you got a good grade in a subject that you find naturally difficult. There are smaller karmic lessons to show or teach you how to handle something as well as significant life lessons that may be ongoing or affect you emotionally. Maybe you have someone in your life that you would qualify as a "frenemy." Someone who's kind of your friend, but you constantly argue or hurt each other emotionally as though you can't help it. That's a karmic relationship. There are also friend-ships where the other individual is closer to you than a brother or sister. That too, is a karmic relationship or a soul mate. Bear in mind, soul mates are *not* just romantic partners, but any person who you have a significant connection with as a family member or friend as well as romance. Why do some people naturally irritate you while others with the same personality traits do not. The simple answer is: karma. The collection of people closest to you is called your "soul family." This could or would be your parents, siblings, closest friends, romantic partners, and in the future your spouse and children if that's the path you are meant to take. A member of your soul family may also be a spirit guide helping you from the other side during your life now or in the past. Again, we are both teaching and learning from each other. We are both healing and helping each other to grow.

Now, the path to healing karma and growing spiritually is through the use of the Law of Forgiveness. You must bring yourself to a place of complete forgiveness for any wrong you have experienced, and self-forgiveness for any wrong you committed to others and yourself. Forgiveness is the path to unconditional love and healing. Unconditional love and healing is the path to divine love, peace, abundance, joy... I could go on...harmony, enlightenment...you get the picture. The Law of Forgiveness works only if you can truly feel the love in your heart for the situation, person and yourself. You manifest what you feel emotionally. Even if your words are of forgiveness, if your feeling is not, then the situation is not forgiven or healed fully. And, it doesn't matter what the other person does or says, in forgiving them you are healing yourself. You may also use the Law of Forgiveness even if you are not completely aware of everything you need to forgive – issues that you may have carried over with you from a past life. The absolute wonder of it is the tremendous feeling of unconditional love that starts coming through when you begin forgiving and releasing that anger, sadness and hurt. You could be carrying anger and emotional pain that you can't relate to in this life, but you carried over from previous lives in order to heal it. Healing it with decrees and prayers of forgiveness is so powerful that you will feel relief as these emotions are released, allowing the good stuff to come through such as joy, peace and harmony. In the ongoing process of healing our karmic relationships, there will be a shift in your perception of people and situations. It will be as though you see through to the other side of things. You will begin to feel compassion for those who used to get you angry and frustrated, because you will realize that whatever unpleasant things they say and do to others, they are doing a hundredfold to themselves on the inside. They are truly unhappy, angry and fearful. Behind all negative words, actions and feelings is fear.

As you've probably read in the first six chapters, you know that you were not meant to walk this path alone. You have been assisted and surrounded by loving support your entire life. Your spirit guides, and guardian angel have been helping you all along even though you may have been unaware of them. As you begin working directly with them through developing the use of your intuition, you will find them tremendously helpful and supportive through all your difficult challenges, situations and experiences. They will also be there to cheer and celebrate your triumphs.

Let's take a moment to look at reincarnation from the standpoint of the religions. Many of you who are reading this book were brought up with some kind of religion. All the various Christian faiths and Judaism have a hard time acknowledging the fact of reincarnation. In the Dark and Middle Ages, any reference to reincarnation in the Bible was removed because the Pope and church leaders felt they needed to control their congregations and followers into living the way they thought one should live. So, what's happened is these changes and teachings carried on into modern day. But, if one truly thinks about it, there's so much evidence within ourselves to prove that reincarnation exists. For instance, we all have preferences and affinities in how we dress, foods we like, activities we enjoy, quirky items we may collect, certain books set in places that feel familiar or enjoyable, an ease in learning about a particular culture's history. For instance, many years ago when I was still working in the publishing industry, I was on a business trip in Dallas. During some down time, a couple of my co-workers and I went shopping at a local shopping mall. While I was browsing in one particular store, I came upon these beautifully, hand-painted Russian nesting dolls. They were almost $300 for a set of six nesting dolls. I am not Russian, had no connection whatsoever to Russia, yet I have always liked these dolls, and so I had to purchase these expensive dolls that had no relevance to my life. I also have a strong connection to anything Mexican: food, country, people, and most of all music and dance. I am of Italian and Czech descent – not even remotely Mexican. I especially love the dancing and music. I absolutely love Middle-Eastern food, love the style of dress from Ancient Egyptian times, the jewelry, the history. All these different affinities and preferences are a compilation of all my past-life experiences. You carry these memories in your cells as emotional patterns. You can also have aversions – places or cultures that absolutely turn you off. Perhaps it was a traumatic lifetime that is coded in your DNA, and created a memory pattern that you carry with you now.

Your dreams can be reincarnated excerpts from specific lifetimes. They will feel differently than regular dreams. You can have a spontaneous past-life recall or strong reaction to a movie you are watching or a particular friendship will bring on a feeling of past-life memory. It's all valid and true – not imagined. The reason they might occur this way is because you may need to gain some insight in order to heal an emotional issue or pattern that has resurfaced in your current life. Allow it to come through in order to learn from it which ultimately leads to healing the pattern. Again, this is another area that you can explore through meditation journeys.

Lastly, before I close this chapter, I'd like to take a moment to address those of you who have come to earth at this time who do not carry karma and life lessons, but have come for an entirely different reason. You may know people or be able to identify yourself as being a little or a lot more gifted and more spiritually oriented. You may be one of the beautiful and loving beings that are incarnating on the earth for the first time that have come from other universes. If you are one of these people, you chose to come to earth to assist humanity and the planet in raising their consciousness and the vibrations of all on earth and earth itself. In order to fit in, you would have spent time training and preparing for an earth life by being imprinted with certain experiences, personality traits and characteristics in order to fit in with the family and life you were planning to have when you were born. You are "light workers." You are evolved souls who have arrived relatively karma-free with the purpose of helping humanity. It doesn't matter whether you choose to become an electrician, accountant, teacher, technology professional or street cleaner. Simply by being here you are helping to raise the vibrations of people who come in contact with you. You may or may not be aware of the fact that you carry this service. Learning to meditate and doing it regularly will help you connect to your spiritual support in order to understand what you are meant to be doing and why with more information and detail.

In closing this chapter, I'd like to say that no matter what happens in your life, there are no mistakes. Everything that happens to you is okay, and if you are open to viewing your life and the experiences and challenges you face with the attitude of **acceptance**, your life will be less stressful and more harmonious. You will also be well on the way to healing your karma instead of creating new karma that you will have to pay off in the next life. Everything is happening as it should be even if it doesn't seem that way. You are both student and teacher to all you come into contact with, family or foe, friend or stranger. Learning to accept the hiccups and bumps in the road as easily as you accept the successes and happy moments will serve you well.

Part II

Your Divine Purpose

Chapter 8

Divine Beginnings

The door was opened to the concept of divine purpose in a few of the chapters in Part I of this book. This section will focus entirely on this concept because it's the reason why you are here; why we are all here. Divine purpose is the blueprint of our entire lifetime. Each time we are born into a new life, we prepare and map out our entire life. Everything is included in this blueprint including our parents, other family members and friends, talents, abilities, strengths and weaknesses, life lessons, relationships of all kinds, physical or health profile, career choices (you may have more than one), the desire to marry and/or have children or not to marry and all the challenges and obstacles that you need to overcome in order to heal karma or pay off karmic debt. In this chapter, we will go into specifics on the many different areas that form your blueprint and divine path. Suffice to say, nothing happens by accident; all is by divine design.

So, this chapter will methodically break down the components of what would be part of the divine blueprint of your life including: choice of parents and immediate family members and manner of birth, childhood health and life challenges, adult health and life lessons, friendships and romantic relationships, innate abilities, talents and skills, educational and/or career and professional leanings, marriage and family...or not, personal challenges and obstacles to handle, health and emotional life lessons, divine service, spiritual path and support and manner of death. Knowing that you may be as young as 13 and probably no older than 23, there will be some details of your divine plan that aren't in the picture yet, but as you have followed your inner guidance to read this book, chances are from here on, you will be better prepared for how to handle life's challenges as they come up, knowing full well that everything happens as it was meant to. You will make mistakes, many mistakes, but how we deal with them, pull ourselves up and overcome them – that's the way we learn from our life lessons. That's how we advance on our path spiritually.

To better illustrate how a life might be mapped out, I have created a story with two main characters, our heroes of the story. First I would like to introduce, Sanaa, whose name means: bright or radiant, and Liam whose name means: strong-willed warrior. They are fictional characters who will meet at some point in this fictional story to illustrate the example of a life featuring many of the aspects of a divine blueprint.

Choice of Parents, family members and manner of birth

Briefly mentioned in Chapter 7 of Part I was the idea of not just soul mates, but having a soul family. This term is broader than the literal meaning of family. Soul family can, of course, include your parents, siblings, cousins, and other extended family, but, it can also include friends, romantic partners and even people we will work closely with at our future jobs. For the moment we will focus on your birth and childhood. So many decisions went into just this part of your life. When you are still a spirit on the other side planning your life with your spirit guides, teachers and ascended masters, you are considering a lot of different aspects of your incoming life. There will be karma you need to heal that was either not healed in a previous life, or the karma was created and you now need to balance it in this life. Karmic debt is karma you owe to someone else from a past-life deed that caused harm in some way in a previous life by you to another. You make an agreement with the soul/spirit of your parents as you are planning your life. They will have been born several years prior to your birth of course, but their spirit or soul energy will have access to this knowledge even though they don't consciously remember planning this part of their own divine blueprint. You even influence your parents in your choice of name. They do have Free Will and we do not always feel we have the name we wanted, but depending on how important your soul felt about a specific name, chances are you have the name you planned to have before you were born. Karmic lessons can also connect with the manner in which we are born. Was your mother's delivery of you difficult, extraordinarily painful, or were there complications in the delivery? Was your arrival early, late, welcomed with joy and happiness, or sadness and reluctance? What race or ethnic culture were you born into? Was your father present? Is your mother a single parent? There are a great many reasons for any combination of situations that could be that not only connect to life lessons, but emotional patterns that are brought forth from many previous lifetimes that still need to be healed. If an issue is healed, it will not ever need to be revisited again. So you only come into a life with life lessons that have not been healed or dealt with successfully. Let's begin our story of Sanaa and Liam.

Sanaa and Liam – Parents' Background

Sanaa: Her parents were very excited about the idea of having a baby girl. Before she was born, her parents had to deal with challenges of coming from very different cultural backgrounds. Sanaa's mother is African-American with her parents being immigrants from the country of Kenya, and her father is white with a traditional American upbringing and background. They met in college, fell in love, and got married despite misgivings from both sets of parents and decided to live in a suburb of Chicago. Sanaa's future two sets of grandparents had serious concerns surrounding the vast cultural differences between Sanaa's mother and father. These differences were not important to Sanaa's parents, and so they prevailed and got married despite the push backs they received throughout their engagement. The most important thing though, was that they loved each other, and were excited about planning a family. Sanaa was the first child and happily born to these two loving parents who would nurture and care for her every need... Maybe too much so.

Liam: *Birth was not planned. His mother was uncertain and scared about being pregnant because she was not married, and wasn't planning on staying with Liam's birth father. Liam's parents' relationship was casual and pregnancy was not the intended outcome. Liam's father did want to have a role in his son's life...or so he claimed at the time of learning of the pregnancy. We shall see how that unfolds. Liam's mother was to remain living with her mother (Liam's grandmother) in Queens until she could stand on her own feet financially...which may or may not happen.*

Now we can analyze the setting for Sanaa's and Liam's birth scenarios. There is already a setting and experiences in place for their arrival. After each story segment there will be a karmic analysis of what was going on pre-birth that was put in each character's divine plan/blueprint.

Karmic Analysis

Sanaa's parents are educated immigrants with strong ties to their native homeland. Sanaa has chosen parents who are loving and nurturing. Her parents will be tolerant of cultural and racial differences, but they will influence Sanaa in other ways. Also, their lovingness will turn into over-protectiveness and this will not allow Sanaa to feel comfortable having new experiences, trying new things because of fear of the unknown. As you can see, Sanaa's put into place a karmic childhood situation that she will have to overcome in order to learn that life lesson and heal the karma. Sanaa has had lifetime after lifetime experiencing fear and failure each time she tried something new. Her fear prevented her success, and thus created a constant cycle disabling her ability to progress in many ways. It stunted her growth emotionally, mentally and spiritually. It's not surprising that she will be small in size physically as we will come to see. This is clearly a karmic life lesson as opposed to balancing karma towards someone you wronged or who wronged you.

Liam's: In Liam's case, it's about balancing karma. His parents are not married, do not love each other, and are financially limited. Liam will be raised for the most part by his mother and grandmother. There will be no consistent male father figure in Liam's life. This is karma Liam has to learn from because in a previous life, he was not particularly loving or kind to his mother nor women in general. He treated woman without respect or kindness, and in order to balance his karma, he will have to learn how to love and appreciate his mother and grandmother as they will be the main source of love, nurturing and care for him.

Sanaa and Liam's Birth Experience

Sanaa's mother's pregnancy goes along smoothly. She knows she's having a girl and together with Sanaa's father has picked out the ideal name. The meaning of the name is very important, and they feel the name "Sanaa" was perfect. She will be their bright and radiant star.

Liam's mother's pregnancy is fraught with a lot of minor discomforts, much like the mental and emotional attitude of his mother throughout the pregnancy. She, too, knows what sex her child will be because her minor pregnancy hiccups forced the doctors to do some sonograms during the pregnancy to make sure everything was going okay. She learned she was having a boy and decided to pick a traditional Irish name – Liam. She felt he needed a strong name to help cope with the challenges of life. He was to be strong physically and mentally just like a warrior. Her view of life was that it was hard and you had to fight for whatever you wanted.

Sanaa: The birth of Sanaa went smoothly. Sanaa appeared healthy and strong, with a penetrating and intelligent look in her eye as if she was aware of everything.

Liam's mother went into labor earlier than she expected and was rushed to the hospital to deliver a premature baby — born 4 weeks early. He needed to remain in the hospital until he was big and strong enough to come home. Liam's mother's recovery from the delivery was challenging, but having Liam in the hospital allowed her to recover fully before he was ready to come home with her. Although she was very nervous about being a new mother, she truly loved her baby boy. In the neonatal unit at the hospital, the nurses noticed that he was a fighter, and he responded very well to their care. Liam's mother was there as much as possible so Liam felt her love when she was there. He was ready to leave the hospital sooner than they expected and able to begin growing up in Queens with his mother and grandmother.

Karmic Analysis

Sanaa: The details of Sanaa's birth would indicate an excellent start. But, we shall soon see in the next section that all is not as it seems. The good news is that she has two loving parents who will do everything they can to nurture her. They will soon learn what kind of parents they will need to be.

Liam: Liam's premature birth and awareness of the pregnancy and delivery have already set the emotional tone to his natural nature. The emotional pattern that life is hard and you have to "fight" for everything is already set. Based on emotional patterns set in his past lives, he carries that forward through the kind of birth he has, and through his experience in the neonatal unit hospital. Again, though his mother is scared and wary of parenting, she does really love him. Liam will learn unconditional love from his mother that she didn't know she had in her. From that loving bond, he will teach her many things as well.

Sanaa and Liam: Childhood Health and Life Challenges

Sanaa: At the age of six months or so, Sanaa's parents began to notice something awry with Sanaa. She never reacted to loud sounds, didn't look up when her name was called. They took her to the pediatrician who tested her hearing, and then from there a specialist who determined that she was born with a type of hearing impairment. Her parents, the loving people that they were, immediately began researching programs, technology and therapy to see what they could do to help their daughter. They wanted her to have as normal a life as any other child, but that would prove to be a bit challenging. They learned how to use sign language, and hearing therapists taught them how to teach Sanaa. Sanaa was in educational and therapeutic programs throughout her young childhood years. She was a very bright little girl, with an aptitude for academic learning. Everything academically came to her easily. Her parents being so overprotective would not let her go to a regular elementary school. They had the means to pay for a private-school education and so they chose to put her in a private school for the hearing impaired. Sanaa was not completely deaf; she wore hearing aids, and as was typical of someone who's challenged in one of the five senses was able to use her other senses more efficiently so it was not immediately obvious to an outsider that she was hearing impaired until she spoke. The manner of her speech was different than a hearing person. It sounded clumpy, awkward and at times difficult to understand unless you knew Sanaa. Nevertheless, her parents insisted she go to a school with children who were just like her. That worked out fine for a while.

By the time Sanaa entered junior high school, she begged her parents to let her go to a regular school. Finally they gave in, but with concern that she would be made fun of because of the way she talked, that she would feel lonely with no friends, and have trouble navigating a noisy school building, Sanaa wanted to go anyway.

Liam: Liam was in perfect health despite his premature birth. He was bright, inquisitive, and had a natural athletic ability too. This was helped by his size and body type which was strong and muscular. He had intense blue eyes, a quick wit and a quick anger. He loved his mother very much but hated that she always appeared weak and victimized. She was mostly victimized by his grandmother who was a stern maternal figure. It also caused him not to respect her the way he should. Liam was always defiant, and not wanting to listen to her. Grandma could be belittling to his mother; it was not meant to hurt, but it did anyway. She was trying to foster a sense of independence and strength in Liam's mother, but it seemed to have the opposite effect. Because Liam's mother seemed unable to turn her life around, his initial anger was directed at her. He would hold it in with no way to express it. Adding to this was the fact that his school friends had a lot of material things and went places that his mother and grandmother could not afford. Although he made friends easily, he also had a chip on his shoulder and always felt different than his peers at school. His athletic ability and good grades, though, afforded him a certain popularity with the other kids. They just never wanted to get on his bad side. This pent-up anger would cause some physical effects throughout childhood. He often had sore throats and terrible colds. He also got painful stomach aches that caused him to miss school. His favorite school subjects were science and math. These subjects were black and white; emotions, in his mind, didn't come into play, so he enjoyed the mental relief from his turbulent emotional mind.

Karmic Analysis

Sanaa: Some of Sanaa's karmic lessons are unfolding. She has a physical challenge of a hearing disability that will cause her parents to become extremely overprotective. Their overprotectiveness is creating unfound fears whenever she tries to break out of the norm and try something new. They express their fears and these soon become Sanaa's. Karmically, Sanaa has planned this disability in order to create the overprotective role her parents take, in order to play out her fear of the unknown. She set the stage for this situation in order to successfully overcome this issue. She's also physically very small and petite. This adds a layer to her fear as she feels that she's very small. Her handwriting is small. Her voice is low and difficult to understand because of the hearing disability. She often plays alone at home because she doesn't know how to make friends easily even though she's at a school with children just like her. But, there's an unrest in Sanaa and she wants to break out. She senses she's missing out on a lot, and is now reaching out to her parents to help her make some changes.

Liam: As with Sanaa, Liam's childhood is unfolding according to his karmic blueprint as well. He has a mother who loves him dearly, but isn't strong enough to stand up to his grandmother; isn't strong enough to fix her life so she can stand up on her own financially. His grandmother, though she loves him, is unable to show it, because of her stern disciplinary nature. She's had a tough life, and tenderness and nurturing are just not part of her character. This has caused Liam to build up unresolved anger at both of them. He's naturally gifted in sports, has a sharp mind that allows him to get good grades in school, and he's discovering a inclination towards math and science because he feels they give him a mental and emotional break from a very "emotionally gray" world. His love for his mother is buried under the anger, and he doesn't respect her or his tough grandmother. This is giving him a negative picture of women. He feels they are weak or mean. His father, though well-intentioned at the time of the pregnancy – has made a life for himself and often forgets Liam. This affects Liam in a very subtle way, as he's learning that you can just walk away from a situation with no responsibility or repercussions.

Sanaa and Liam: Immediate Family Members

Sanaa: Now Sanaa's parents had two more children after Sanaa. She has a sister two years younger and a brother who's six years younger. Neither of them has disabilities. She loves her siblings, but has a close bond with her sister. Her sister is very sympathetic to how Sanaa feels, and is the complete opposite of Sanaa. She's a free spirit, which can be very challenging to her parents who have set the tone of overprotectiveness since Sanaa's birth. Sanaa admires her free-spiritedness and wishes she could feel that carefree. Sanaa's sister admires Sanaa's smarts. Her sister has to work harder for the good grades, but is fortunately gifted artistically. Sanaa's brother is typical of most little brothers. She finds him annoying, immature and always in her stuff. They bicker and bark with no patience for each other. Her brother likes to come up and startle her, and is often successful in catching Sanaa unguarded. This automatically feeds into Sanaa's inclination towards fearing the unknown. You can see the pattern manifesting in many different, synchronistic ways. Sanaa absolutely hates it when her brother does this. He loves to get the reaction from her that he does. Sanaa also has a very large extended family on her mother's side. They have big family get-togethers where they eat traditional African dishes, laugh, play music and have fun. Her father's side is more reserved. Except at special occasions (like a graduation or birthday) in Sanaa's and her sibling's lives, the two families don't tend to get along very well, nor are very tolerant of each other, so there's a natural division between the two sets of grandparents and families. This adds to Sanaa's stress and at times lonely feeling of isolation and being different. She loves both parents' families and wishes everyone would get along and be loving to one another.

Liam: is an only child. Since his mother could never get her life together and out from under his grandmother's nose, she never got married, and so was very careful not to get pregnant by accident *again. His mother had two older brothers who were married with families, but he didn't get to spend much time with them as they lived far away. And when he was with them, he felt isolated and lonely because he couldn't relate, but was secretly jealous of his cousins' "normal" family life. Because of his self-imposed isolations, his uncles and cousins didn't know how to connect with him even though they tried and wanted to know him. He couldn't break free of the pent-up emotions that he guarded constantly. He doesn't want to have these other tender emotions, like needing love, kindness and compassion. He has them, but he feels it's weak to show them, so he closes himself off.*

Karmic Analysis

Sanaa: As you can see the emotional patterns that are already part of Sanaa, have layers in a synchronous way. Her brother scaring her feeds into her fears. In looking at her brother, he plays a small role in helping her live out the karmic life lesson of which she will need to break out of in this life. Perhaps in a previous life, she was strong and intolerant of weaker people and maybe taunted the previous incarnation of her little brother. The process of karma's checks and balances is very complex. In all situations, everyone is in both the role of teacher and student. Having a big family is wonderful, but again another dimension is added that feeds into Sanaa's loneliness and isolation. This mirrors her feelings about herself and her hearing disability. What follows in the next chapter will illustrate that what you think and feel becomes your reality. If you want a different reality, you must change your thoughts and feelings.

Liam: Like Sanaa, Liam also feels loneliness and isolation, but the root cause is very different than Sanaa's. Liam's anger and inability to express emotions other than anger isolate him. He's angry at what he doesn't have and is unable to value what he does. He can't see the love his mother has for him because it's colored by his anger at her weakness and inability to stand on her own two feet in order to give them both a better life. Not being able to connect with his uncles and their families adds another dimension by again, showing him what he doesn't have.

Summary

Often times, our childhood experiences and environment condition us into the emotional life patterns that we must heal and triumph from. As a child, and even a teenager, you do not yet have the tools to overcome these limiting feelings. When you are very young, everything is viewed by how it affects you. As you get older, you begin to realize that others have feelings and your behavior can affect them as well, but as you are still not an adult, it's difficult to perceive things more objectively. Throw in some adolescent hormones and things just go haywire – exacerbating the ingrained emotional feelings you have been feeling all of your life. Yes, some children are born to more supportive and nurturing parents who can then become parents who can teach their child and teenager how to mature emotionally, but most parents are still trying to figure all it out themselves. And, I can tell you from experience as a parent – many times we don't learn or realize what's going on inside of us until we have children. Personally, I feel blessed to have figured out a lot since having my children and it's my hope that they will grow up more balanced, happy and peaceful.

Chapter 9

Innate Abilities, Talents, Skills and Educational Leanings

We all have talents and abilities that seem to already be there. These gifts are meant to help us in our divine service, our divine life purpose. How we utilize our talents will determine the quality of our life. For instance, denying our talents and passions is harmful to our spiritual well-being as we chose these abilities to assist us in our mission on earth. Every single person is here for a reason, and has a mission to serve humanity. When we choose not to fulfill what is in our hearts (because it is our hearts that remind us what we are supposed to be doing here), then we have not fulfilled our divine plan, nor served in raising our good karma that will advance us on our path to higher service.

This next section on the story of Sanaa and Liam will focus on them discovering their natural talents and abilities in high school while also dealing with limitations, obstacles and the creation of new negative karma. Any life is perfect in its imperfections and mistakes are learning opportunities as you will see as you read on about our two heroes.

Sanaa and Liam: the Challenge of School Life as a Teenager

Sanaa: Now moving into Sanaa's teenage years, we can see how her natural talents, abilities and attraction to certain academic subjects is beginning to reveal itself. Sanaa has always been super smart when it comes to school and academics. She has an ease in learning and retaining information. She loves books, and has been discovering a talent for creative writing. She loves to read all types of books, mostly fiction, from the classics to books set in modern day. Because of her hearing disability and loneliness, she goes into the world of books. They feed her soul's desire to have adventure. This desire has manifested in her asking her parents if she can start high school in a regular school, not the special school for hearing impaired. They wounldn't allow her to do this in junior high, and now she's pursuing this again. Her parents are extremely reluctant — reminding her constantly of how it could be a failure, what could happen and how she might feel about these things. But, she persists and they give in with reservation. So, she begins at the local high school in her town, with trepidation and fear. She is very shy, and at first people don't realize why. They misunderstand her shyness for arrogance and aloofness. When they finally hear her talk, the other students are at first taken aback. They are not used to being around someone who is clearly very different than them on the outside. Most people just leave her alone, but when she must speak up in class she can hear snickering in the classroom of other classmates laughing at her voice. Because of they way she speaks, her words are difficult to understand. This makes her feel very self-conscious, and she feels isolated even more. On top of that, the teacher becomes impatient with her because she's different and has trouble speaking clearly, so she doesn't feel 'safe' in school. No one is there to help or protect her. This continues to feed into her fear. She must conquer this fear in order to be successful in a traditional school environment. Each day is harder than the previous day. But, there's going to be a silver lining, a crack of sunshine to begin to turn her school life around.

Liam: He too, begins high school and puberty has really kicked in and is affecting him emotionally. It has exaggerated his anger, and he has outbursts over nonsense and is often times quite short-tempered and impatient. Because he's naturally athletic, playing sports has become an outlet to some degree. It allows him to let off some steam so he doesn't become a pressure-cooker ready to blow. Liam's favorite sport is basketball. He loves the fast pace and his naturally large and muscular size makes him a very capable player who learns the strategies of the game easily. The coach and his teammates love his enthusiasm and it's the one place he feels like his real self. He doesn't choose to have much to do with the girls in school. He thinks they are silly, dumb and full of themselves, caring only for make-up, clothes and boys. He also is a good student – particularly with math and science. He knows that in order to break free from his upbringing and the constant feeling of not having enough, he needs to get a good education. So, he takes school very seriously, very seriously. His mother never has to remind him to study; never has to complain about getting good grades. He has a couple of friends he hangs out with who he knows he can count on, but still nobody gets too close. His mother feels this remoteness and she feels helpless in trying to figure out how to get close to him. She doesn't fully realize the extent of his dislike of her life situation. This inability to connect with him in any real mother-son relationship along with her difficulty in standing up to her mother and become financially independent begin to show signs of affecting her health.

Karmic Analysis

Sanaa: We are seeing a continuation of their karmic emotional and life challenges continuing to develop at school. Sanaa has taken the first steps to healing her fear of the unknown. In past lives, she was unable to be successful in conquering her fears. In this life, she has put into her divine blueprint some assistance for herself to prevent failure. If she realizes success in this school environment, it will ripple positively for the rest of her life. She will continue to be tested on her fears, but since she will be able to reflect on her high school years as being successful, she can constantly reassure herself that success is possible if she stays the course. Also, her success here will help teach her parents to allow her daughter to make decisions – that she could be successful based on her persistence. They will begin allowing her to weigh in on decisions about her life and not make all the decisions for her.

We are also seeing the beginnings of some talents through her passionate love of books. This love of books is serving multiple purposes. First, it's driving her desire to live an adventurous life through the stories she chooses to read. Second, her love of books has stirred a feeling in her to create and write her own stories. Third, it is a restful outlet when she needs to recharge and regenerate herself in order to continue making the decision to go to school each morning.

Liam: School life is okay for Liam. He's carved a little niche for himself between the classroom and basketball. Puberty has kicked in, and his anger is unpredictable. He continues to not care much for girls or women in general, with his mother at the top of the list. He gets good grades, does his homework, and is academically responsible so he feels she should just back off. He's not learning what he needs to learn in his relationship with his mother. He's adding more negative karma with his terrible attitude towards his mother. And, it's continuing to spiral downward, because he doesn't realize how this is affecting her health. He doesn't even notice how pale she looks lately. Grandma is more like a father figure than a kindly grandmother, and he hates the way she treats his mother even though Liam doesn't treat her very well either. So, in seeing that, there's a spark of love within Liam that we shall see if it becomes more.

Liam's love of math and science are the beginnings of him looking to the future as to what he will choose to study in college. He thinks he would prefer a career that's dominated by men so he doesn't have to deal with emotional women, but we shall see.

Sanaa and Liam: How Easy it Is to Create Karma

Sanaa: Within a month after Sanaa began school, just when she was just about to give up and give in to her parents being right about attending a regular school, she made a connection with another girl. She mustered the courage one day to join a club. It was a writers' club where students could spend one afternoon a week after school doing creative writing under the guidance of one of the English teachers. While participating in this club one week, she met another young girl who was friendly and kind. This person stood up for Sanaa when someone snickered at her manner of speech when she was sharing an idea for a creative story theme. When Sanaa looked at her gratefully, the girl smiled. That was the beginning of Sanaa's first friend at the new school. In one brief moment, this new friend created a shift for Sanaa that allowed her to consider staying at the school. The blossoming of this special friendship also sparked another gift. Sanaa was very, very funny when she felt safe and confident enough to talk. Others at school started to pay attention and realized that Sanaa was witty, and sometimes made the most hilarious comments. When Sanaa realized that people were laughing with her, and not at her, she was thrilled. School wasn't so bad anymore.

Sanaa was doing well at school now. She had friends, a social circle, good grades in school, etc. She began to let it all go to her head. She thought she could do or say anything and everyone would think her funny and fun to be with. She would often use her wit to put down other people thinking they would understand that it was all in good fun. This continued for a while, and often people would not have that positive reaction. When they indicated they didn't like her humor, she just dismissed it as them not having any sense of humor. She then began to use her sense of humor to become more popular, thus ostracizing others that didn't like her wit and sense of fun. This went on for a good portion of her tenth-grade school year, until one day, she said something witty, and cruel about a girl from her class. This girl happened to be passing by when Sanaa made the comments about her. The girl was instantly crushed, and began crying. Sanaa, at first, insensitively scoffed at her tears, saying it was a joke and the girl shouldn't take everything so seriously. Other people around Sanaa were agreeing with Sanaa. This really upset the girl, and she ran off in a fit of tears and emotions. The girl was so upset that she wasn't paying attention to the school driveway, and got hit by a car. Everyone ran outside to see if she was alright, and the girl was very badly hurt. Sanaa was horrified at the thought that she was the cause of this girl's accident. While she was realizing her role in this accident, all the other students who were laughing with her, turned on her and blamed her for being cruel and mean. Sanaa went home feeling really heavy and regretful about her behavior. We shall see in the next passage how she handles her mistake.

Karmic Analysis

It's very easy to create more negative karma. We get caught up in our human life, our egos try and often succeed in taking the lead, and we end up hurting others and generating negative energy and karma. Now, there's a couple of ways Sanaa could handle this situation. She can learn from it, and begin to make amends to the young girl she hurt. Depending on how she does with making amends, she can heal the negative karma she created with this other person in this, her current life. Or, this could carry over as something she has to heal in her next life. Healing karmic debt can manifest in a great number of ways. For instance, the girl who was at the receiving end of this experience could very well have created this situation from which to balance and heal her own karma. Perhaps this girl needs to balance her karma by having this experience because she was the cause of hurting another individual in a previous life. Perhaps she caused this to Sanaa in a previous life. Karma, healing karma, balancing karma, life lessons, karmic debt…it's all so complex, and because we interact with so many people on a day-to-day basis, not to mention all the people we will associate with, meet, spend time with, interact randomly with throughout our lives. We are affecting each other in ways you can't imagine. Every little thing you do, say, and feel has an effect on people, energy around us, and the earth itself.

Liam: As we get back to Liam, he too, is creating more negative karma through his disrespectful relationship with his mother. His mother is getting paler and weaker physically. She's begun missing work a lot lately, and Liam has been oblivious to all of this going on around him. He continues to dismiss his mother as inconsequential and an annoyance until he comes home from school and finds her collapsed on the kitchen floor, unconscious. There is no one home, so he calls 911 for an ambulance to take his mother to the hospital. His heart is feeling soft twinges of pain and worry. What is wrong with her? Still refusing to feel any emotion of love, he waits until his grandmother comes home to tell her what happened so they can go to the hospital together to find out what is wrong with his mother. He behaves very coolly and very removed emotionally. A lot is going on inside of him but he is dismissing it in his mind because he still doesn't want to feel anything like love to her. He's thinking, "She's going to be okay, it's nothing. She'll be fine and everything will return to normal." But, will it?

Karmic Analysis

Let's look at Liam for a moment. He's been dealing with his issues regarding women since he was born. His life lesson in this area has been unraveling as he moves through his young life; as his mother, and grandmother continue to prove his theory about women. What he needs to learn is that unconditional love heals everything including himself. But, he's not ready yet. This jolt of his mother's illness will also put his mother on alert about her choices and attitude about herself, but Liam has a role in helping her too if he chooses that route. If he does not, he will not have fulfilled his karmic debt to his mother, nor will he have overcome his own emotional limitations. You can see how their divine blueprints are interwoven where both are teacher, healer and student. Let's see how he does in the next segment.

Sanaa: Sanaa, being a compassionate person by nature, takes this error in judgment to heart. She realizes that she lost her way and was not being her true self. Being in the unique position of having been at the other end of mean or unkind words and actions, she now realizes what she's done not only to the young girl who is now in the hospital, but also many others who may have been hurt by her words. Sanaa decides to visit the hospital to apologize to this girl and begin to make amends. The girl has a lot of bumps, bruises, a concussion and a broken leg. Sanaa decides to visit regularly. She is lucky in that this girl has accepted her apology. Sanaa knows, without anyone telling her, that she needs to do more than apologize. When the girl leaves the hospital, Sanaa decides to assist this girl in her everyday life until her leg is mended and she does not need assistance anymore. A friendship develops between the two girls, and they discover how much they have in common. Sanaa is profoundly changed by this new friendship, and makes an unspoken decision to treat everyone with kindness and compassion. She also realizes in this relationship that most things are not what they appear to be on the outside. You can never know everything from appearances. Lastly, she learns that profound healing comes from forgiveness. This girl truly forgave her, and both of them benefited from the tremendous healing that took place from this genuine feeling of forgiveness. Sanaa took a little longer in forgiving herself, until she realized that what came out of this accident was a friendship that would never have taken place if the incident hadn't happened. Sanaa, being a thoughtful person, is beginning to open up to new emotional concepts that she's blessed to learn from through this girl and their friendship. Sanaa has just begun her spiritual journey though she's unaware of it, and doesn't know much about spirituality.

Karmic Analysis

Because Sanaa has chosen to make amends, by taking seriously the repercussions of her actions, she has opened up a new pathway that is now available to her according to her original divine plan. She has also healed the karma that she created now, instead of in the next life. It is my belief that we have many roads on our divine plan, but not every path is the same. That it depends on the choices we make. If we do not make the choices that flow with our divine plan, then certain pathways of advancement and opportunity will remain closed at that juncture. If another similar opportunity for growth occurs later on, and we succeed in healing it then, then a branch of that path will allow us to access the untrodden portion that was inaccessible before to us. We can continue our upward journey. If you think of your life as a constant serious of "forks in the road" with forks in the forks, and side roads that lead backward and forward, you can see how complex our divine blueprint is because of the free will that we have living on this planet. At this particular point in Sanaa's life, through this new friend who is more spiritually advanced than her, she has an opportunity to open up to her spirituality.

Liam: *His mother is diagnosed with leukemia. Liam is having a hard time comprehending what this means, since he's stuffed most of his emotions deep down inside of him. He's angry at her for being sick, but secretly worried that she will die. He begins to suffer from terrible stomach aches. There are knots in his stomach and he's having trouble eating. His grandmother is taking care of his mother at home now. His mother is on medication and doing all sorts of cancer treatments to fight the leukemia, but his mother is depressed and doesn't have the strength or will to fight it as strongly as she should because her heart is so sad and heavy. She longs to feel loved and nurtured. His grandmother wasn't very nurturing to his mother, and he didn't allow his mother to get too close to him either. She is holding on to her own anger at the way her life turned out as well. This is why the cancer entered her body. Liam continues to stay locked away and removed from what is happening with his mother. She continues to get sicker, weaker, paler and sadder each week, month, until she needs to be hospitalized for the extreme pain she is feeling from the cancer. All traditional treatments of the leukemia have been unsuccessful because of her mental and emotional state. She dies quietly in the hospital in the middle of the night with neither her mother nor son around her. Liam is devastated, and goes into a rage as the pent-up emotions and anger surface in an explosion. He destroys everything in his bedroom, and when it's over, he's depleted emotionally and physically as he falls asleep in a heap on his bed. The days following, he and his grandmother prepare for her funeral, bury her, and return home to an emptier house. Liam feels empty inside and a sense of guilt; of opportunity missed. But, he doesn't know what he missed doing, just that something wasn't done that was supposed to have been done.*

Karmic Analysis

Liam, unlike Sanaa, did not heal karma through a relationship with his mother. Even when she got sick, he was still stuck and angry emotionally. His mother, too, did not heal her karma by overcoming her lack of nurturing and loving support from her mother. And his grandmother perpetuated her own negative karma by never being flexible and open to changing even though she had witnessed the results of her actions through her daughter's illness and death. Liam is still young, only 18 years old, in his final year at school. He will have future opportunities to learn to express emotions like love, patience, tolerance and compassion. He will not be able to heal the karmic debt to his mother in this life, but he will have a chance to heal himself if he allows and accepts opportunities for growth later on.

Sanaa and Liam: Overview of Talents, Abilities & Skills Moving Forward

Sanaa: During her school years, Sanaa discovered a number of talents and gifts that she plans to develop in college and ultimately through her career. She loves creative writing, with the added benefit of a tremendous wit and humor to her stories. She's beginning to open up spiritually and that has given her not only emotional strength, but is helping her continue to overcome her fear of the unknown. She learned that she can make a difference to people. So, she's also interested in psychology and helping people as well. Additionally, with her hearing impairment, she's discovered an outlet in the form of dance. Feeling the vibrations through music and movement gives her body and spirit joy and relieves stress and increases harmony in her life. She particularly likes vigorous dance like tap dance because she can feel the vibrations better than with ballets and waltzes. She plans to major in writing at college with some minor courses in sociology and psychology. She is accepted at Northwestern University in Chicago.

Liam: *During Liam's school years, he discovered his love of math and science. Also, he's very athletic and enjoyed playing junior varsity and varsity basketball. Basketball was his saving grace as it became a physical outlet for his anger and stress over his unhappiness about his home life and his lack in life. He didn't have a lot of friends, just one or two who "got" him. The death of his mother in his senior year drives him to be completely focused on getting good grades and doing well athletically so he can leave his unhappy life behind through becoming financially successful and rich. He never wants to do without again. He gets a basketball scholarship to attend Northwestern University in Chicago. He majors in astronomy as well.*

Karmic Analysis

Sanaa and Liam: As you can see, in discovering what they are good at, what abilities and leanings they have towards a profession, they both end up at the same college in Chicago, Illinois. They will meet at some point at college. Everything is unfolding as was planned in both their divine blueprints. You see Sanaa and Liam are also part of each other's soul family.

Summary

This chapter began the focus and transition from childhood to adulthood including educational direction for future career plans. Also, our hero, Liam, had to deal with the loss of his mother. This is a layer that helps form his direction and educational leanings. Nothing exists in isolation, and everything contributes to the greater whole. If Liam had overcome his anger towards his mother, perhaps he would have stayed in New York to get a college education. That would have put him on a slightly or greatly different path. Would he have still met Sanaa? If that was their plan before they were born, then yes. Their guides and angels would have found a way for them to meet a little later; perhaps when Sanaa arrived in New York for her job. Or, maybe another path would have opened up since he made different choices earlier on. That's why it's important to realize that there are no accidents. Even with the gift of Free Will, nothing happens that wasn't supposed to happen for an individual, a group, or a situation. Many, many times when something didn't turn out the way we had hoped, we think if only I had done this, or they had done that, or chose this person to do it better, or that situation to create a better outcome. You can drive yourself nuts going over and over and over different scenarios in the, "would have, could have, should have" category, and to what end. You can't change the past. But, you can *learn* from it, or simply *accept* the outcome as having happened exactly as it was meant to be. When we accept a situation even if we don't like the outcome, we actually begin to look at it from a different perspective. For example, several months ago, I chaired a committee for an elementary school event. The members of my committee were volunteers who requested to be on this committee. I had quite a diverse number of moms and personalities in this group. When we began meeting, it became quickly apparent to me that there were going to be some challenges and I was beginning to regret chairing this committee. When emails started flying back and forth that had a certain negative tone, I could have immediately reacted defensively in the same manner I received the emails. I could have thought, "Why are these people on the committee?" The "If only so and so didn't decide to join this;" or "If only I hadn't chosen to chair or be part of this committee" began to happen inside of my head. The "would have, could have, should have" drama was beginning to depress me and take over my thoughts. Being the spiritual person that I am, I realized that there was a life lesson in this, and I didn't want to fail in this opportunity. So, I cleared my head, took a deep breath, and replied to their emails with respect, kindness, genuineness and validated their concerns and suggestions. This was not false, but a determination to view this through my heart and not my ego. So, I did not take the defensive, but instead focused on the fact that despite how it appeared, these difficult moms wanted the same thing I wanted, which was a productive and successful program for our kids. When I replied to their emails with respect and compassion in my heart, I turned the situation around. When I validated the other members' ideas and concerns and suggestions, I got their best talents, skills and commitment. One of the members who started off with a combative attitude became friendly, helpful and supportive. By leading everyone with respect and valuing their input and ideas, we ended up having one of the most successful programs of its kind ever! What you can derive from this story is every day you get to make choices. Choosing to view your life through your heart and not your ego will always be the right way to go. As you can see, I too, still have to make that choice every day. Some are harder than others you will find. Making decisions from the heart instead of the head/ego, will lead you to advancement in your spirituality and your divine path.

Chapter 10

Friends, Romantic Partners and Others in Your Soul Family

Your soul family is not just the people and family you are born into, but many members of your soul family you meet as childhood friends, and others moving on into your adult life as well. Not all of them are meant to be with you for your entire life, but they will be with you for a portion of time in order to heal karma, karmic debts or serve in life lessons that you chose to experience in this lifetime. You will have any number of romantic relationships from one or two significant ones to many more depending on what your soul planned for you to learn. Romantic relationships can be soul-mate relationships, karmic relationships or twin-flame relationships. Friendships can be the same way.

In the beginning of your adult life no matter whether you attend college or immediately go into the workforce, you will form adult friendships, have romantic relationships and if you are working will also form bonds through being with co-workers or colleagues together depending on your working situation or profession. Often times, bonds can be formed through your job, particularly in service professions like teaching, nursing, the police force, fire-fighters, etc. because of the camaraderie of these professions where you share similar experiences of helping people.

There are many, many ways, though, of meeting people who will become part of our lives and the universe is quite creative in forming ways and opportunities for us to meet the people we are meant to have in our lives. Being open to the unusual ways, such as random meetings in a grocery store, a public park, through a third-party introduction, even blind dates, can have an impact on our lives in either a positive or negative way. All are healing, and learning opportunities.

Now we shall see how Sanaa and Liam progress in this area of life.

Sanaa and Liam: Forming Friendships at College

Sanaa: Sanaa fortunately lives close to Northwestern University and is able to take public transport to school each day since she does not yet drive. This is because she's afraid to drive because of her hearing disability. Since she has some hearing, and it's amplified by her hearing aid, there's not a problem if she makes this choice. Later on, she will get another opportunity through someone's help to consider learning how to drive. In the meantime, she has taken a deep breath, and a big leap by going to a big university to study writing. More new people to meet, more new experiences, gives her both an exhilarating and scary feeling as she starts her freshman year at school. But, this is college, not high school, and she soon realizes that people are not going to quickly make fun of her because of her manner of speech, but she must continue to conquer her natural inclination towards shyness to take advantage of opportunities to make friends. It will again be her sense of humor and wittiness that draws people to her. Everyone loves to laugh, and this time though, she has learned not to use her gift of wit to hurt people's feelings. She makes a great use of irony and even her professors enjoy her humor.

She begins to make friends with other students who are majoring in writing. She does not need to work because her parents are financially able to pay for her schooling, so she can be completely focused on her education. But not having to work allows her some free time to make social connections and even begin dating. In her sociology class she meets a young man who she finds very handsome, with kind eyes. She catches his eye, and they connect. After arranging for some dates over coffee with other classmates, he asks her out on a date. Thus begins her first romantic relationship.

Liam: Has started his freshman year as well at the same university as Sanaa, but they move in different circles at school and will not meet just yet. He is totally and completely focused on his studies and basketball. He must take a job off campus to supplement his scholarship in order to get by. He doesn't mind, and he finds work at a pizzeria delivering pizzas around town. They are flexible with his school schedule especially since he is such a conscientious and efficient worker. Having to drive around delivering pizzas allows him to really learn the area. He enjoys the wide open space of suburban Illinois which is very different from the cramped and crowded area of Queens where he's from. He doesn't have too much free time to make friends, but nevertheless, his athletic ability makes him popular with some of the other basketball players. And, because he's also very smart academically, some of the players ask him to tutor them in various classes. He makes additional income from that and he finds he likes helping people a lot. They are so responsive and appreciative of his care in tutoring them properly, that he begins to enjoy tutoring and seeing people get better school grades because of him. He gets his first taste of being in a position to make a difference in an individual's life. This gives him his first inkling of feeling real emotions of kindness, compassion and caring.

Karmic Analysis

Sanaa: Sanaa has a good start at school. She's made some friends, started dating a nice guy, and is allowing her talents and abilities to shine through her writing talent and and sense of humor.

Liam: His guides have lovingly set the stage for him to effect positive change within himself while being away from Queens and his roots for a while. He's studious, focused and has found a new talent in helping people through his tutoring service. There are a few specks of light shining through his closed-up heart.

Sanaa and Liam will not meet for a while as they need to have other experiences first. Those experiences will ultimately be the cause of their meeting. You can see some of the layering of their experiences as their lives unfold through the backdrop of their upbringing, emotional limitations created in order to have life lessons, as well their own conditioning through a compilation of all their experiences from infancy to now.

Sanaa and Liam: Continuation – Relationships & Personal Development

Sanaa: School is going well for the most part at Northwestern and so is her relationship with the young man. She is in love for the first time and enjoying the feeling. She is really enjoying her writing, and feels very secure that she chose the right path of becoming a writer. Her dream is to write books about people, their everyday lives told in stories delivered with humor and warmth. Her sociology and psychology classes are providing in a way that will help her with character development in her future book writing. She's formed friendships with a circle of four other women and they get together regularly for dinner, coffee, movies, etc. She also spends time with her young man whenever he gets a chance to break away from his arduous schedule of pre-med classes. He wants to specialize in pediatrics down the road. He's also taking extra courses in psychology and sociology as well. Her life is moving along very nicely. Two more years pass at school and she's enjoying the summer before her senior year at college when her young man whom she has been with through all of her college years thus far makes an announcement. He has an opportunity to finish up his senior year at Stanford University in California. They have a special advanced program in pediatric medicine – the area he wants to specialize in. It's an opportunity that doesn't come along very often, and he's just as upset about leaving Chicago and Sanaa as she is. She is under-standably upset, but realizes that he needs to do this. He knows he's going to be working and studying really hard while he's in California and suggests that they break up, feeling that if they are meant to be together, they will reunite later on. If not, he doesn't want to hold her back from meeting someone else. She doesn't want to do this, but he insists that it's better for both of them. They will still keep in touch by phone and remain good friends. Regardless, she's heartbroken. He leaves in August before school starts for both of them, and she has a couple of weeks before going into her senior year waiting for her heart not to hurt so much. She knew she was considering going to New York after college and so they would probably have had to part anyway; it just happened sooner than she was ready for.

Liam: *Two years have passed for Liam as well. The tutoring, having opened up his heart a little, has made him aware of his loneliness. He decides to start dating – nothing serious – but he just wants some company to not feel so lonely. The girls he asks out are nice enough, nothing that makes his heart want to pursue anything past a date or two. They are just a diversion to keep the loneliness at bay. He's 21 years old now and someone he meets through the pizzeria asks if he would like to become a driving instructor. He knows the area so well, and they are looking for instructors that could drive to the far reaches of the county without getting lost. He enjoyed tutoring so much that for him it seems like more of the same thing. Teaching people how to drive might be fun.*

They arranged for him to take an instructor's course over the summer, and he began working as a driving instructor in the fall. It worked out perfectly with his hectic school schedule because again, he could set his own hours to teach people how to drive. In the last three years he did make one good friend. This friend also had an astronomy major and they enjoyed spending time at the local plane-tarium, studying together and working on projects at the library. This friend was the only person with whom he shared any stuff about growing up in Queens with his mother and grandmother. Liam felt he could trust his friend to not make any judgments. His friend, despite everything, could see that Liam actually had a good heart. He saw it in the way Liam talked about tutoring and how some students got an A because of his help. His friend could sense the pride and joy in his voice when he talked about his student. Seeing that Liam loved tutoring so much, he suggested that Liam consider taking some classes in education this coming senior year; maybe even doing his master's degree in education. Liam said, "No way" but secretly tucked it away to think about later on. His friend saw something in Liam that Liam doesn't yet see in himself.

Karmic Analysis

Sanaa and Liam: The spirit guides and angels have assisted in helping Sanaa and Liam's divine plan intersect in this final year of college. They both needed to have their own experiences in order to be ready for meeting on the level they will meet now. Their divine plan has them ultimately getting married and forming a family. Sanaa, though, needed to have had a meaningful relationship so she would recognize the difference in what her feeling for Liam would be, and Liam's life is entirely set up in order to meet Sanaa, and be ready to open his heart. His heart has already been opening through the tutoring and even a little through his casual dating. It's paved the way for him also to recognize the significance of their meeting.

Sanaa and Liam: A Divine Meeting

Sanaa: *The school year begins and Sanaa is starting to feel better over the relationship being over. She buries herself in writing, school and her family life at home. She makes some time to hang out with her friends, but mostly she keeps her mind very busy to help her get over the relationship. At the beginning of the school year, her professor selects her to take an opportunity to intern for a famous author who lives in downtown Chicago. It's a terrific opportunity she thinks, but realizes it will only work if she has a car and can drive. Her parents offer to give her a car if she finally gets her license. Her fear of driving is now competing for her desire to intern* *with this author. She must give the professor an answer, and she has until the end of the school year to learn how to drive, pass her driving test and get a car. The internship would start the following summer. With the loving assistance of her guides, she accepts the opportunity through her professor, and now has to set out getting driving lessons. She sees a flyer at school for driving lessons. How lucky is that? She's thinking, "Coincidence?". She calls the number and sets up her first lesson on the coming Saturday morning.*

Liam: His senior year started, Liam decides to continue with his current major and chooses not to add any courses in education. He does, however, begin working as a driving instructor. His knowledge of the area and city continues to grow as he's sent in all areas to pick up his students for their driving lessons. He posts flyers at school to let people know that he is a driving instructor, though he thinks most people at school already know how to drive. He still feels compelled to post flyers anyway. Much to his surprise, he gets a call from a student at the university. They arrange for him to come to pick her up at her family's home for Saturday morning.

Sanaa and Liam: It was pouring with rain on the Saturday morning of Sanaa's first driving lesson. Fifteen minutes before her scheduled appointment, she planned to call to reschedule the lesson, but Liam arrived early and just as she was calling, he was at her door. Too late, she would have to follow through. In her mind, she thought he was very nice-looking but kind of stand-offish. In his mind, he thought about how small in size she was and would she be able to see over the windshield. He got behind the wheel first to drive to a safe location to begin lessons. Since it was raining, he thought going to a large, empty parking field would be better than trying to drive on local streets. She was relieved and agreeable to that idea.

Though neither of them wanted to admit it, there was a degree of chemistry in the air, and their close proximity to each other in the car made it more palpable. He thought she had beautiful eyes, and amazingly soft and smooth skin. He heard her unusual manner of speech due to her hearing ability, but since he was not accustomed to reacting to things like that after tutoring so many different people over the last three years, he had no particular reaction. Because he didn't react to her voice, she began to relax and feel comfortable around him. He felt safe to her, and she knew it was very fortuitous that she found his flyer about driving lessons. As was her usual self, she began to use her sense of humor, and it had the desired effect. Liam laughed and since he wasn't used to laughing very much, laughed even harder. It was a great release to be able to laugh. He didn't expect to feel so good from laughing. If he wanted to feel better, he always turned to sports, to basketball. Now, he found such enjoyable relief in laughing, and this lovely, tiny girl was the reason. The attraction was definitely mutual. Already, in a brief time, they were both getting something they both craved. He needed lightness and joy in his life, and she need to feel safe to try new things.

By the end of the first lesson, he found himself asking her on a date. She started to hesitate, thinking she wasn't over the other guy, but suddenly decided to accept. They arranged for him to pick her up on Sunday night for dinner. They also arranged her next driving lesson for the following Saturday. The rain stopped, and he had her drive carefully and slowly back home. He walked her to the door, and they parted when she went inside.

Karmic Analysis

Sanaa and Liam: As you can see, everything is falling into place. They are already benefiting from meeting. Both of their emotional worlds are being opened and soothed in healing their karmic issues. This relationship will have ripples on all the levels they need to learn and heal from. At times it will be a beautiful blessing and at other times it will challenge their very beliefs. These were beliefs that needed to be challenged and changed in order for the two of them to grow. Although this story doesn't have near the depth and complexity of our actual lives, it has enough detail for you, as my reader, to see how everything is intermixed, interrelated, and connected in mental, emotional and divine ways. You can also see how the spirit guides, angels and divine teachers assist us, provide the tests and opportunities for us, but don't do the work. They suggest in our minds to encourage us to do what we are meant and planned to do. Let's see how their lives unfold in this romantic union.

Sanaa and Liam: A Beautifully Divine Romantic Partnership

Sanaa and Liam: This meeting marked the beginning of a life-changing divinely created relationship. They enjoyed their first date tremendously. Liam laughed so much it left him breathless in more ways than one. Sanaa thought he was so handsome, strong, and smart. He was soooo different than any other guys she met. She loved his piercing blue eyes, his big strong hands, and she enjoyed the feeling of safety *just by being around him. The significant relationship with the other young man allowed her to now realize that there were new depths of feelings one can have when meeting the right person. Sanaa and Liam began dating regularly. Over time, Liam started to realize that maybe not all women were weak or mean. He noticed that although Sanaa was petite in size, she was not weak in character. She was not dumb, but extremely clever and funny. He was intoxicated with her ability to make him laugh. That laughter opened up feelings he didn't know he possessed, and it allowed him to begin to trust expressing them. She was so kind, loving and compassionate. To him, she felt both fragile and powerful at the same time. There was a level of safety there for him as well.*

We will fast forward their romantic relationship knowing full well that they both realize they belong together; that this relationship is leading them towards marriage. Decisions they both make that keep them in Chicago surround the fact that they are supposed to be together. With his loving and meticulous instruction, she passes her driving test, gets a car, and begins her internship with the author in the city. With Sanaa's help he realizes his own talents; decides to do his master's degree in education after all. And so the relationship continues to blossom and strengthen over these two years as they both need to be there for combined and separate reasons. In that time, Liam must face some inner truths about himself as he feels his own transformation through his relationship with Sanaa and his growing interest in teaching. He makes amends with his grandmother and tries to visit her more often and to be present when he is there. She is still a tough, restrained and unemotional woman, but she does let him know she appreciates his efforts. He's changed, so she has changed around him.

Karmic Analysis

Karmically, they both need to be in Chicago for a number of reasons; for their career, for their personal growth, and ultimately for their relationship to go towards the direction of marriage. In the between-life state of planning this lifetime, they both agreed to be loving soul mates and spiritual partners. Together they learned through bumps and stumbles how to heal some of their life lessons. Sanaa learned how to overcome some of her fears of the unknown. The biggest block being her fear of driving with a hearing disability. Liam began to open up his heart on many levels. Having Sanaa there to assist him in a loving, non-judgmental way allowed him to trust himself with these feelings. It was hard and along the way in their relationship, he had bouts of anger and resistance. He would pull away from Sanaa. She would feel the loss and lack of emotional support at that time, but it also allowed her to begin to trust herself more when being on her own during the times that Liam would pull away. He was doing his own healing process – feelings that he shut down years before as a child, and failed to resurface when his mother became ill and subsequently died. Them both having to be in Chicago for those two years following graduation at Northwestern, allowed the rollercoaster flow of their relationship to develop at its proper pace. This formed a very strong foundation and intimate knowledge of each other from which a strong love grew between them. No relationship is perfect like in the movies. The strength of a love is tested constantly and relationships are hard but when you bring out the best you can be within each other then everything you go through is worth it because you become a better person when you are with the right romantic partner. In this fictional story, the universe worked with both Sanaa and Liam to help them help each other, and therefore it helped all others around them. Were mistakes made and feelings hurt during this time? Yes, absolutely this happened. In addition to each other, they had strong friendships on both sides to assist their relationship and personal lives along with way.

Chapter 11

Career, Marriage and Children

Our lives have a depth and interconnectedness that is far more complex than you can imagine, and this story of Sanaa and Liam is merely an example of how certain life lessons, choices of Free Will, and karma might play out as planned through our divine blueprint.

To marry or not to marry, to have children or not, where to live, what job to take based on which profession you would like to pursue are all choices made in combination with each other as a decision in one area will undoubtedly affect all the other connected areas of one's life. For our young couple, marriage and children were a choice they agreed upon. It was in their divine plan, and we continue their story with their decision to marry.

Sanaa and Liam: Marriage and Career OR Career and Marriage

Sanaa: After completing her internship in Chicago, opportunities presented themselves as possible choices for Sanaa to pursue her dream of being a writer. The author she worked for in Chicago became her professional mentor and encouraged Sanaa to begin writing – to just start writing and see what comes about. At around that same time Liam was completing his master's degree in education, Sanaa received an opportunity to work as a junior editor with a book publisher in New York City. This was arranged by her mentor, and again Sanaa was faced with dealing with her "fear of the unknown." This was good timing though, because Liam was completing school and didn't feel he needed to stay in Chicago any longer. It seemed like divine providence that they were both ready to leave and since Liam was from New York, it made perfect sense that Sanaa should take the job in New York City.

Liam: Liam completed his second degree and decided that he wanted to become a teacher. With Sanaa having the opportunity to go to New York with a job waiting, Liam decided to act on a BIG decision. He decided to propose to Sanaa so they would be engaged when they returned to New York, and he would feel more comfortable about deciding to live together during their engagement. Her parents approved of him, and he enjoyed the big family life through being part of her family get-togethers. This was another healing balm for his disconnected emotions and so he hoped they would be receptive to the idea of him getting married to their daughter. He adored her and couldn't imagine a life without her by his side.

Sanaa and Liam: Liam proposed and she ecstatically said yes. She loved the idea of moving to New York and living with him. She knew her parents would be better able to deal with her moving away and living with Liam knowing that commitment of marriage was in place. Her sister cheered her on – seeing how Sanaa was growing and changing in leaps in bounds all in a positive direction. She came to love Liam for that reason.

To fast forward their story a little, they did marry in Chicago having planned the wedding long-distance with the help of Sanaa's family. Her parents paid for the wedding and Liam's grandmother flew out to be welcomed by Sanaa's parents and family. It was a celebratory and memorable time for the couple, and afterwards they settled for a weekend honeymoon in New York City. This was all Liam could afford and he insisted on paying for the honeymoon. Sanaa didn't care; just being with her new husband was enough. Liam got a teaching assistant's job in a local Queens school until he received his teaching certification from the state. He enjoyed teaching at the elementary-school level and the kids brought out his tender, nurturing side. Sanaa did very well as a junior editor at the publishing company where she worked, and completed her first novel. She was waiting to see if and where it could be published.

They delayed having children for a few years while trying to *establish their careers. Liam's grandmother began to soften as she spent more and more time with Sanaa. Sanaa's natural sweetness, her quiet and gentle nature, and how she brought so much laughter and happiness to Liam was the reason. Deciding to live with his grandmother, Sanaa and Liam were taking a big chance after all of the hard years growing up. Sanaa insisted because she saw the need for Liam to heal his relationship with his grandmother. This, of course, would ripple through to healing him from the loss of his mother. Liam also began to relish family get-togethers with his uncles and their families now, and he didn't feel so lonely and isolated thanks to Sanaa and his improved relationship with his grandmother. They were enjoying a happy life for the most part as many couples enjoy in the first few years of marriage, particularly before the arrival of children. Sanaa's book got published, Liam got a teaching job as second-grade teacher in a school in Queens, and their life was just about perfect. They considered moving to Manhattan since the success of Sanaa's book increased their financial income substantially, but felt they didn't want to leave his grandmother. Instead, they stayed in Queens and moved into a new, nicer and bigger place where there was room for his grandmother to live with them. About four years into the marriage, Sanaa announced she is pregnant. Everything was about to change.*

Karmic Analysis

Sanaa and Liam: Life is going fairly smoothly for both of them. Why not? Not every moment in a life is about dramatic experiences. There were everyday occurrences that had to be dealt with. Liam was still dealing with old anger patterns. It affected his health. We will get into that in Chapter 13. Sanaa was still somewhat introverted, but being in publishing constantly challenged her to being more adventurous socially; particularly since there were so many press events to promote books and authors. They argued, and hurt each other through their arguments from time to time. It wasn't always easy for Liam to live with his grandmother given their history, but still thanks to Sanaa it was much better than during his childhood. One issue that hadn't been fully healed was Liam's distaste for weak and/or needy women. This will be tested in what happens in Chapter 12. With any divine path, there is preparation for what is to come next. Nothing happens by accident and we can be guaranteed of one thing – change. That is the only guarantee and when we embrace change, and accept it as part of our life's purpose and life lessons, we can live much happier. When we do not, that's when our life lessons challenge us, instead of us challenging them. In the next chapter, we will see bumps and obstacles as they embrace parenthood, death of family members and illness.

Chapter 12

Personal Challenges, Obstacles and Health Lessons

It's important to truly understand the nature of life challenges, obstacles in your path, drama, crisis and the like because everyone has these situations no matter where you grow up, how much money you have, what you do for a living, and how much love and support you have in your life. Things go wrong, accidents happen, life happens – that's the way of all human life. So, this chapter is devoted to a period in the life of Sanaa and Liam to illustrate these bumps in the road.

Looking at our life as an adventure, as a rollercoaster with ups and downs, as a journey with dark and lighted pathways will put you in a position of viewing your glass as half full. Everything has a purpose; everything is a lesson for you or for someone else on your path. Everything happens exactly as it's meant to, and there are no oopsies. You cannot learn anything from success or perfection. You can only learn from mistakes, difficulties, and obstacles. Each triumph over these mistakes and difficulties results in advancement spiritually. Even individuals who don't see themselves on a spiritual path will enjoy personal fulfillment, success and satisfaction from knowing they handled something and overcame the challenge or obstacle. That alone advances you. If you deliberately approach your life as a journey to grow, heal and handle your life lessons and karmic debt spiritually, you will advance also, but with a specific goal and a definite direction. Both are choices of Free Will. As a reader of this book, you are probably on the spiritual path to God. There is no greater journey than one towards harmony, love, balance and wholeness for that's what you receive when you make that your destination. Now let's see how our lovely couple handles their bumps in the road.

Sanaa and Liam: Personal Challenges

Sanaa: At the announcement to Liam and her family about her pregnancy, everyone was elated. Parents usually love hearing that they are going to be grandparents. This was no different with Sanaa and Liam's family. Everything was moving smoothly. Sanaa experienced many of the early pregnancy symptoms of fatigue and morning sickness. She didn't mind. They were living comfortably financially, and both emotionally and economically they were ready for a baby. They began shopping for the baby's nursery. Sanaa's family in Chicago were making plans for her baby shower, and everything was moving along nicely until Sanaa began experiencing early labor pains during the fifth month. She immediately went to her doctor to find out what was going on. Liam went with her. The doctor ordered complete bed rest and ceasing of all activities, like work, shopping, traveling, etc. "Okay," she thought, "this is just a little hiccup in my plans, but the baby is going to be alright."

Liam: Understandably Liam was greatly concerned. He went to the doctor with Sanaa and when he heard she had to be on complete bed rest until she delivered he was both relieved that Sanaa and baby were okay, but it triggered his pattern about weak women. Though he didn't fully comprehend it at the time.

Karmic Analysis

There are two karmic events going on here simultaneously. First, Liam's negative emotional pattern is triggered. He is, at first, very understanding about Sanaa's situation. He gets her home, sets her up with care. Sanaa's mother has agreed to come and help since it's now too much for his grandmother. After all these minor preparations for Sanaa are set up, he then has the mental time to process what's going on. This begins a serious downward emotional spiral that pulls him away from Sanaa just when she needs him most. The other event that's intertwined intentionally so is the fact of the baby choosing this situation for Sanaa and Liam. This situation is also triggering Sanaa's fear of the unknown. She now needs the safety of Liam, and he pulls away. The baby is both serving as teacher as well as student in this scenario. The incoming spirit of the new child has lovingly chosen to help Liam and Sanaa work out some more karma in healing their individual life lessons. Liam did not learn this lesson earlier in his life through being with his mother, so another opportunity has been given him to heal again. From external appearances, all of this seems like a big problem, nuisance and complication, but from the inner spirit side, it's anything but. If Liam chooses to overcome his negative pattern and choose his great love for Sanaa, he has an opportunity to permanently heal this negative pattern and life lesson. For Sanaa, it will move her along, as she has placed on her path constant challenges to continually deal with her fears in a great many ways. All indications show that she will succeed as she has before in all the other events in her life. Liam has failed in this area a few times. Let's see if they are able to overcome this issue.

Sanaa: *At first, Sanaa is a little worried about Liam's coldness and remoteness. As it persists, she's worrying more. This is not good for her and the baby. She suffers more contractions at around six months, and again the doctors are able to stop them, but they are concerned about her stress level as is Sanaa's mother. Fortunately, her mother is very supportive and wise. She doesn't fully grasp the whole situation, but is sensitive enough to see something is going on within Liam that has nothing to do with her daughter. She lovingly tries to help. Her mother having faced her own challenges of marrying a man of another race and culture has had her share of issues in life.*

Liam: One night, Sanaa's mother begins trying to connect with Liam. He's abrupt, rude and closed off. She persists and he loses his temper, bangs furniture, breaks dishes and makes quite a ruckus and then storms out of the house to cool off. Sanaa is visibly upset and goes into spasms of labor pains and begins to bleed. She's rushed in a taxi to the hospital. Her mother leaves a message on Liam's phone, and then travels to the hospital to be with her daughter. Liam doesn't get the message for hours. Fortunately he hasn't done anything reckless. He went to find one of his childhood friends from high school. Someone he can trust who also has a family and understands the stress of becoming a father. Liam breaks down his silence and spills years of anguish. He's finally facing the emotional loss of his mother amidst all his inner turmoil. It's overwhelming. His friend listens without any comment. He's just a silent sounding board for Liam's emotional outpouring. During this crisis, Liam runs the gamut of all his emotions until he is completely drained. It's at that moment he finally has his revelation. Most important is how much he loves his wife and unborn child, and also how much he actually loved his mother. His guides have been connecting with him this whole entire night lovingly supporting him, and gently guiding his revelations. When he realizes everything, he leaves his friend's house and rushes home only to find no one is there. Now he thinks to check his cell phone messages and realizes that he might be too late. He rushes to the hospital, finds out where Sanaa is and races to her hospital room. She has been admitted and they are trying to stop the contractions. She's only six and a half months pregnant. He rushes to her side to ask forgiveness; tells her he loves her and that he has finally figured out some stuff which he will tell her about another time. He profusely expresses his love and commitment to her, and she lovingly accepts his explanations. The baby's heartbeat returns to normal, the contractions finally subside, and Sanaa is feeling much better. She will remain in the hospital for a couple of days, but it appears the danger has passed.

Karmic Analysis

Sanaa and Liam: This was all planned. Sanaa and Liam's guides never left them, but instead aided them through this crisis. Sanaa's guides provided healing and comfort to Sanaa while Liam's guides assisted him towards realizing his negative emotional pattern was causing all of the stress and anger since Sanaa learned that she must be on bed rest. Liam was having what is called a healing crisis. They can be emotionally tumultuous and messy, but when it's over and there's understanding and clarity, it's amazing how quick healing takes place. The baby planned this experience for herself as well. It sets the tone for the baby's karmic patterns to come after birth.

Sanaa and Liam go on to have a healthy delivery with no more issues. She has a beautiful baby girl. Grandparents, uncles, aunts and other family are overjoyed to welcome this little one. Moving the story along, Sanaa and Liam go on to have two more children without incident. They end up dealing with a lot of the usual karmic and everyday life lessons of parenting three very different and active kids. The children display their own karmic patterns, life lessons, relationship challenges between each other, etc. Sanaa and Liam learn the hard way, the way all new parents learn in how to care for their children. They learn that you can't use one way for handling discipline, structure and love for all of your children. What works for one child might have the reverse effect on another. I'm sure you can relate to this on a personal level since you are still living with your parents and siblings.

What has happened with Sanaa and Liam is they are realizing that their children are very different in many ways than other children. Their children are exhibiting gifts of intuition, spiritual leanings, empathy and healing abilities that they don't understand. All of them have had learning challenges and some physical development challenges as well which ties in to the reasons why they are gifted. Fortunately, they begin finding ways to learn about their special and gifted children. This will put them on a deliberate spiritual path which will change their lives. This leads us to other karmic life lessons in this next section.

Sanaa and Liam: Obstacles on the Path

Sanaa and Liam: Their youngest child has had a lot of health and developmental issues since birth. As an infant the baby had food allergies and skin rashes. She was very sensitive to sounds, and was easily startled by sudden noises. She didn't sleep well at night, up frequently. Later on, she developed slower than her peers, not talking very much even at age two. She seemed clumsy with her movements and use of her big and small muscles. By preschool, she was receiving speech, occupational and physical therapy to bring her development on par with others her age. But, aside from all the physical stuff, she was a beautiful and unique spirit. She was naturally attuned to God, and asked a lot of deep questions you wouldn't expect a child of four or five ask. She would ask things like, "Grandma, what makes you happy?" and expected a real answer. She asked questions about God, Jesus, and angels. The child was also very loving and affectionate, but was also extremely sensitive to other people's energies. It made things hard when she became overwhelmed in a crowded or noisy place like at a party or a busy store. She would often have to be removed from the environment in order to feel better. Sanaa and Liam found themselves having to change the way they parented with this youngest child. Everything they had done before with their other two children did not work at all with their youngest.

By the time this little girl was old enough for elementary school, her parents didn't feel she was as ready as they would have liked. In order for their daughter to succeed, they needed to make sure teachers, parents, therapists, and special education teachers under-stood their daughter's specific needs, gifts and challenges. When their daughter was still a baby, they went to their regular doctor for her care. She got her shots, was given medicine for her frequent ear infections, and a lot of traditional medical intervention. Nothing helped, but instead got worse. It was about this time that Sanaa's friend introduced them to holistic medicine and more natural means for taking care of their daughter. Just when they saw something improve, another symptom appeared.

Fortunately, Sanaa worked from home since she was a book author, and was able to be there for all the meetings in order to get her daughter what she needed at school to succeed. Sometimes she was denied services for her daughter, and had to appeal to get those services. Her daughter was difficult when it came to things like homework, reading and writing time because these things were hard for her daughter. It was about this time in Sanaa's life that she decided to investigate things like yoga and meditation for herself and her daughter. The little girl was always asking the big questions like, "What's a guardian angel?" and "What happens when I go to Heaven?" This forced Sanaa and Liam to evaluate their beliefs in God, in the doctrines of their religious background, etc. Sanaa began reading a lot of books. She read books to improve her daughter's health naturally; books for personal growth and books for spiritual growth. As soon as she began doing this type of soul searching and questioning, things began to happen that Sanaa couldn't explain, like spontaneous past-life recall, coincidences that were too coincidental to ignore, spiritual dreams, and her feelings becoming more fine-tuned. Her little girl continued to have challenges through first grade where very little of the services seemed to be helping. Her other children felt a little neglected by her because of the attention the littlest daughter received.

In the midst of all of this, Liam's grandmother died. This was particularly hard for their youngest daughter who adored her great-grandmother. This little one had always been able to warm her great-grandmother's heart with her loving affection and sweetness.

Then, Liam lost his teaching job due to budget cuts in the school district, and Sanaa's parents weren't well and she needed to go back *and forth to Chicago to help figure out what her and her two siblings were going to do with her parents.*

Karmic Analysis

All of this and so much more was the backdrop of a complex family life with ups and downs, little and big difficulties, happy and sad occasions. How you handle obstacles, crisis, difficulties and traumatic events is often a reflection on how you look at yourself and your perception on life. Sanaa and Liam's daughter was born with a lot of challenges, and she chose Sanaa and Liam to be her parents to help her through these things. Their daughter was also teaching them a lot about life beyond the physical human life on earth and opening up their worlds to more expansive views of life beyond our humanity. We all have Free Will and it was up to Sanaa and Liam to decide which way to go – deny spiritual meaning and occurrences, or embrace and become more open-minded. Sanaa had gotten a taste of some of this through her high school friend and the experienced helped her now as a parent of a spiritually gifted child. Liam once again, had to learn about nurturing and caring but now from the position of parent. People that were "too sensitive" annoyed or angered him, and here he was raising a little girl who was extremely sensitive. This forced him to evaluate what that meant to him. Why was she so sensitive? Did being sensitive have to mean weak? No, it didn't. Many sensitive people are very strong emotionally. This was a huge learning curve for Liam. Healing a big part of this when Sanaa was pregnant with their first child, paved the way for him to become the loving father he was to his three children with the extra tenderness he needed to exhibit for their littlest child. Sanaa had the bigger opportunity of expanding her ideas about the universe, God, and Heaven. They both rose to the challenges that their children provided them and it changed them forever. There was growth, there were mistakes and sadness, but there were gains and forward movement too.

Ultimately, you will see tremendous growth in Sanaa that will assist her to the end of her life.

Sanaa and Liam: Health Lessons
(This section will be brief as a chapter in Part III of this book will be entirely devoted to health.)

Liam: Several years have passed now. Liam and Sanaa's youngest child is a teenager in high school, and the other two are in college. The oldest is studying at a university that is out of state, whereas the other daughter stayed local and is studying in New York City. For a while now, Liam has been suffering from abdominal pains, fatigue, mood swings, and a general feeling of un-wellness. His regular doctor recommends he has some medical and blood tests done to figure out what is wrong. Liam agrees and both he and Sanaa await the test results.

Sanaa: It becomes more apparent to Sanaa than Liam that something is terribly wrong with Liam's health. She knows the strength, energy and vigor of her husband, and he was never one to take naps, be inactive in the daytime or complain about physical ailments. He is doing all of this now and she's tremendously concerned. He is the love of her life, and now that the children are older, she looks forward to doing more things together; to enjoy their later years with travel, adventure and renewed romance.

Liam and Sanaa: Liam's test results return and it seems Sanaa's gut feelings were accurate. There's every indication that Liam might have liver cancer. The scans reveal a tumor in his liver, and it explains why he has had abdominal pains in that region. They schedule surgery in order to do a biopsy and remove the tumor. Liam is overwhelmed and scared. Sanaa is scared too, but tries not to show her worry to Liam as they prepare for his surgery. His children are all worried, but very supportive, loving and present. He has been a good father overall, even while dealing with his anger issues off and on. Both his wife's gentleness and calm demeanor along with his children have taught him much in regards to healing these issues. Liam has the surgery. They remove the tumor and start him on traditional cancer therapies to make sure all of the cancer is removed from his body.

With all that Sanaa has learned from approaching her children's wellbeing holistically, she realizes that Liam must address his emotional and mental blocks that have caused his physical body to react and get sick. While Liam appreciates and believes in God, he is not particularly spiritual, and has a hard time understanding that everything that ails us, starts with our mental and emotional patterns — including patterns that began from past lives, as well as conditioning and patterns formed and perpetuated in our current life. Sanaa is trying to get him to be open to alternative healing therapies. At first he resists natural means, but then as the chemotherapy begins making him sicker, he finally agrees to try something alternative.

Sanaa first makes changes in their diet as the food one eats can create inflammation and disease if it is highly processed. She helps him to gently begin detoxing his body and liver. This, of course, begins to create unpleasant physical side effects which interestingly enough makes him angry. She then finds a practitioner of flower essence remedies who prepares a flower essence combination blend that assists Liam address certain emotional issues particularly the anger. It appears to make him sicker physically, and make his emotions stronger. It's interesting to note that Liam is now expressing a full range of emotions — something he never did before. At first this is hard for his family to deal with until Sanaa realizes what's happening, and helps her children deal with his erratic mood swings and overly emotional states. He's both physically detoxing and emotionally releasing at the same time. Sanaa coaches him through it, and bites her tongue every time she wants to react defensively knowing that this is a process.

Within a few weeks, the symptoms began to subside and heal. He began to feel better…a lot better. This is the beginning of clarity – a clearer state of mind, body and spirit. He has revelations about things from his past. He has vivid dreams with strong messages. He begins also to feel a sense of contentment and momentary happiness. Because of Sanaa's love, knowledge and emotional support, he is able to transcend his own destructive behavior. His unfailing love and trust in Sanaa is what gets him to maintain the alternative therapies even during the worst days of it. Within six months, the doctors declare him cancer-free.

Karmic Analysis

Liam: So, what was happening to Liam on a karmic and spiritual level? Well, his mental and emotional state finally penetrated all the various layers of his body until it reached his physical body through his liver. The liver is the organ where anger is stored. If you bring anger from a past life into this life, and then perpetuate it through the life lessons you planned for yourself during the between life state, then it's one of the areas of the body where this that can manifest disease. Anger can manifest in other ways as well. (More details of some of the basic emotions and how they manifest as illnesses in the body in Part III.) In Liam's case, he got liver cancer. Once the doctors dealt with the acute situation of removing the tumor from his liver, the process of real healing began when Sanaa introduced alternative and holistic healing options that had a profound effect on Liam.

Sanaa: Liam's illness could have paralyzed Sanaa given her history of being afraid of the unknown. Liam is her rock, her safety net and the love of her life. If her life up to this point had been a series of failures in overcoming her fears, Liam's outlook might have looked a lot dimmer.

Liam: At the same time, if Liam had not made slow, but steady progress in dealing with his anger – particularly during that crisis of Sanaa's first pregnancy – he would not have had faith, love and trust in Sanaa's holistic recommendations.

Sanaa and Liam: This was a final test to some degree for both Sanaa and Liam to show to them how far they had come in healing their negative life/emotional patterns. Liam made the biggest changes and the result was an enormous boost to his emotional healing process. They got through this together because of all the hard work of their many years of marriage and in constantly choosing love; constantly choosing their relationship and family over external influences and negative issues. For individuals like Liam, this is very hard work. It did not have to be that hard. But Liam chose some very challenging karmic lessons to overcome. These were lessons he hadn't learned repeatedly in previous lifetimes, but he finally learned them this time, all because of the love from Sanaa – both as his current human wife as well as the beautiful spirit she was before they were both born. He too, served her well, in helping her heal her fears.

It bears repeating, that constantly choosing the path towards advancement and healing is really what Free Will is all about. The Free Will of both my heroes had them choosing a path of progression. Sanaa's was a bit smoother than Liam because she already had developed a rich, spiritual life. Liam's path was full of snarls, pitfalls, uneven and choppy roadways but he still "chose" to navigate through it. He had helpers in the form of good friends on the human/earth side, and he had supportive spirit guides and angels on the other side that guided and redirected to keep him on the upward path.

Summary

This chapter focused on life's many and great variety of challenges on the path towards the spiritual advancement of joy, harmony and peace. Our couple endured many personal problems, difficulties, loss of loved ones and health lessons together. They planned these negative events to help them heal their karma, pay off karmic debt and learn their earthly life lessons. They also planned for each other not to go it alone, as they didn't need to heal these difficulties successfully by being alone, but by being united together. They built in the fact that by constantly choosing their love for each other over anger, negative influence and their problems, they allowed themselves opportunity for success.

Liam's path could have been easier if all along he had been open to working with his spirit guides, angels and his own God-Self. If you constantly tune in to your intuition looking for guidance, your path, though not snag-free, will be infinitely easier. If you view and deal with everyone nice or mean, good or bad, challenging or easy, with the protection of unconditional love and grace, your life will not only appear easier, but it will contain more everyday joys, moments of inner contentment, peaceful interaction and success in your life hurdles.

You, my beloved reader, who are still so young and at the beginning of your journey have the opportunity to lead your life differently by absorbing the lessons in this book and practicing meditation, intuitive development and just plain old listening to your gut feelings. Hurdles don't have to be nearly as high, obstacles don't have to be nearly as big, and difficult relationships don't have to be nearly as frustrating if you have faith in your intuitive guidance, handle everything with unconditional love and compassion and move forward with a positive thought and emotional state.

Chapter 13

A Divine Conclusion of Life

Free Will is choosing. It's as simple as that. If you live a life that never *gives you the opportunity* of coming out of your comfort zone, then you really won't have lived life. If you live a life where *you never choose* to come out of your comfort zone, then you will have little or no spiritual growth. And, you will face the same issues, challenges and negative patterns over and over and over aaannnnd over again, looking more like a hamster in a treadmill than the beautiful light beings you all are.

Our lovely Sanaa and Liam are in the twilight years of grandparenthood. But, just because they are considered old by human standards, doesn't mean they still can't challenge themselves, and learn new things. No matter how old you are when you learn your life lessons or heal your karma, you will progress. Have you ever heard the use of the acronym of F.E.A.R.? It means **F**alse **E**vidence **A**ppearing **R**eal. Fear is an illusion. We learn fear from personal experiences of failure (Oh, I failed at playing basketball, soccer and baseball so I won't even try tennis, track, or gymnastics.), injury (I fell out of a tree when I was five and I'll never climb one again.) and conditioning from our parents' fears while we are growing up (You can't do that, son, you'll get hurt!). We also bring certain fears of when we are born into our current life that we didn't deal with in a previous lifetime. While fear can teach us many things for a while, holding onto that fear at the cost of never overcoming it, keeps you on the wheel of karma dealing with the same things again and again. Can you see a pattern here? Fear holds us back, and *choosing* to try anyway brings us forward. Let's see how Sanaa and Liam conclude their lives.

Sanaa and Liam: Realizing/Recognizing a Special Divine Opportunity

Sanaa and Liam: They are both in their 70s now. They have seven grandchildren from all three of their children. They live a quiet life in their lovely home in Queens. Liam's cancer never returned. Liam is retired from classroom teaching and is enjoying traveling to see his grandchildren. Only one child lives in New York. The other two live out of state. Sanaa's spiritual self continues to grow and advance. So many doors have opened to her as she's been willing to absorb many spiritual lessons of creating your own reality, staying positive, manifesting abundance in a variety of ways, and living her true self.

So what plans are they making now? Well, plenty in fact. Although they have some minor, age-related health issues, gray hair, far-sightedness, occasional achy joints, and the like, they are very active.

Sanaa: Recently an opportunity has come for them to move to Portugal through Sanaa's publishing contacts. Sanaa has always dreamed of going to Portugal, and so when a colleague of hers said that there was a villa owned by another book author, she brought the idea excitedly to Liam. It was a nice size home walking distance from the beach in the Porto area of Portugal. There would be room for their children's family's to come and visit and Sanaa was open to the idea of learning a new language.

Liam: Portugal seemed so far away from everything familiar. To Liam, this seemed too far away. He liked his comforts and always looked forward to coming home after a trip away. Now the away part would be permanent. He was thinking, "I'm too old for making this kind of radical change."

Sanaa: The villa was very reasonably priced and the money she saved from her book sales over the years would make it possible for them to buy it. Sanaa reassured Liam that they wouldn't have to sell their Queens home in order to purchase the villa. Also, Portugal was truly just across the ocean. Most importantly, Sanaa wanted to keep their romance and relationship healthy, fresh and interesting. Sharing this adventure would recapture all of that youthful sense of adventure. Uncharacteristically, Sanaa was embracing this once-in-a-lifetime adventure with both feet. Her old fears were fading away. Her trust in her inner self had grown tremendously and she wanted to embrace new things with enthusiasm instead of trepidation.

Liam: *Sanaa was winning Liam over. He insisted they see what they were getting into before taking the leap, and so they went to Portugal for a vacation. The air was charged with magic and they became intoxicated with the romance of the country. The villa was going to be perfect for their needs, and Liam discovered that there would be a way for him to explore an old love of his from way back in college when he studied astronomy. There was an observatory with a huge telescope within fifteen minutes of their villa, and once he learned enough of the language, he could work part time or volunteer there to continue his interest and love of the stars. Everything was looking like it could work out.*

Sanaa: *Through all of the work Sanaa has done in manifesting what she wanted, moving to Portugal was the dream come true. There was one hiccup to mar her dream, and that was the fact that they would be leaving their children and grandchildren and living so far away. Her children were stunned at first until they got used to the idea. Her middle daughter who lived near them was feeling it the most because she lived near them, and now they wouldn't be there anymore. Sanaa had to help her daughter come to terms with the idea of them living in another country. She realized that her daughter too, held a fear of the unknown. It was the reason she lived close to them. This daughter was now going to have to learn to stand on her own two feet, rely on herself and choose the marriage and family she created with her* *husband. Sanaa would always be just a phone call or computer face chat away. Sanaa and Liam would visit home frequently, and the grandchildren would visit at holidays and summertime.*

They moved into the villa on Sanaa's seventy-fourth birthday. Adjusting took a little time particularly because of the language barrier, but they both chose to learn the language in earnest. They began to enjoy the lifestyle, and Sanaa even began to write her eleventh novel – which was set in, where else, Portugal.

Sanaa and Liam: *Sanaa was determined to complete her life having no regrets that she didn't fulfill something that was in her heart to do. Living in Portugal was a huge adjustment, mostly because of missing her children and grandchildren. But, choosing not to take advantage of this opportunity, she would have regretted and held on to the decision for the rest of her life. Liam embraced the change even more so because it revived a passion he thought had long since left him. He actually went back to school in Portugal to become an astronomer. Nothing was in the way anymore and he thoroughly enjoyed being in school again and hitting the books. With Sanaa writing and Liam studying, they were truly equal partners who enriched each other's lives completely. Their love affair did take a turn for the better. Their love for each other deepened. They had eight great years before Sanaa was to pass away.*

Karmic Analysis

Sanaa never stopped growing, never stopped striving to get more out of her life. Once she healed her fear of the unknown, it opened her world wider than ever. Liam never had these issues, and so with little real resistance, was open to Sanaa's idea of moving there. Money hadn't been an issue for them thanks to Sanaa's success as an author, so only one thing could have stopped them, and that was fear of not being able to see their grandchildren grow up.

Because of the way Sanaa and Liam turned their lives around

at key times in their lives, times of crisis and overwhelming change, it paved the way for them not to think of themselves as too old for new adventures and change. From Sanaa's inner work and meditation practice, she realized that you only grow old when you stop growing. (Sanaa used many tools of healing that will be discussed in Part III.)

Often times, it's the female gender that's more open to all things spiritual. If you are a male reading this book, you are way ahead of your peers in so many ways. Being spiritual, and having your intuition guide you, and living holistically is empowering, not weak and girly. You have more control over your destiny if you allow your spiritual side to develop. You can have the best of both worlds as long as your intentions are pure and not self-destructive or harmful to others. Liam didn't view his life spiritually, but he completely trusted and loved his wife who never betrayed him, that allowed him to make the leap. Once again, because he chose his partner and stepped out of his comfort zone, he ended up rediscovering an old passion that in his seventies had him going back to school. They still had the everyday problems and obstacles that everyone deals with. The bumps and bruises of life, but overall they approached their life with a positive attitude and attracted that more than anything else.

Sanaa and Liam: Conclusion of Two Lives

Liam: Sanaa died at the age of 82 in a car accident walking back from town after shopping for dinner. It was truly an accident with no malicious intent from the driver of the car and Sanaa died quickly. Liam was lost from the loss of her. He was completely emotionally devastated. He couldn't imagine living without her. Over the years she had become his safety net – when all the time he thought he was hers. He didn't realize this until she died. All of the family came to be with him, and she was buried in Portugal because that's how he knew she would want it. It was summertime which meant the grandchildren weren't in school, so some of the family stayed. The youngest daughter stayed the longest to help her father through his grief. She was extremely sensitive and knew she was needed for a while. She also knew when to leave so he wouldn't transfer his dependence from her mother on to her. She left after a month to return to her own life. As time passed, he slowly found his footing. His children thought he would sell the villa and come home for sure since what brought him there was Sanaa, but he surprised them by choosing to stay. He felt that she was closer to him here than back in Queens. His passion for astronomy also gave him his own personal reason to stay. He made some friends, established some roots, and so created a life by himself. As a matter of fact, it was the first time in his life that he was completely alone. This too, was something new to learn.

He lived to the age of 92 before he passed away peacefully (disease-free) in his sleep.

Karmic Analysis

Sanaa had one more lesson to teach Liam, and it was how to live on his own. It was always planned that she would die first. Although the cause of her death was a car accident, she died quickly and fairly painlessly. Karmically, this was set up in a way that would allow her to leave quickly without the drama of illness. Liam had one last, important lesson to learn. He needed to learn to trust and love himself, and he could only do that by living alone. He had all the wonderful memories and experiences from his life with Sanaa to draw upon during difficult days when he missed her. Her voice would be in his head, reminding him to live lovingly with no anger. He did do just that, enjoyed his last ten years as an astronomer who enjoyed looking out at the vast and beautiful night sky. He saw Sanaa's essence in every beautiful star he viewed through the telescope, her sweet and gentle voice in his head, and her presence in his dreams. He died peacefully with no regrets.

Summary of Part II

This story of Sanaa and Liam hopefully illustrated key points about the divine path, purpose and the whys and hows of us coming to be here on this earth at this time and all the many times before. As you can see, nothing happens by accident.

This story doesn't even nearly contain the complexity of one's life, but it does illustrate in a variety of ways how we came here with lessons to learn, relationships to heal, karmic debt to pay off, and much, much more. This story was intentionally kept to just our main two protagonists, but in any life, there is the layering of teaching and learning as we interact with everyone we meet both intimately through being family and friends, as well as apparently randomly as acquaintances, peers and strangers. We are making decisions pretty much every moment of the day. There are thoughts running through our minds constantly. If your inner dialogue is negative, then that's what you can expect back in from your external environment. If your thoughts are loving, compassionate, and non-judgmental, then you will attract positive experiences more often than not. Since we all have Free Will, there will be times that you will deal with someone else's use of Free Will which might be handled through the vantage point of anger or meanness. Dealing with them with compassion will still have a better outcome than dealing with them with the same level of unpleasantness.

If you have difficult relationships with your mother, father, brother, sister, school teacher, soccer coach, etc., it's important to realize that we are all mirrors for each other. What is it about you that attracts that behavior from that person? When you evaluate and correct or heal yourself, the other person will seem to have changed. Therefore the nature of your relationship will have changed. The only person you can ever change, heal, correct or improve is you. Your protective layer is actually your force field of unconditional divine love.

I conclude this chapter with an exercise you can practice every day or when you know you will have to deal with someone that typically upsets you and makes you feel defensive and uncomfortable.

Exercise:
You do not need extensive preparation to do this exercise. It's something you can do to start your day, and then you can fortify it throughout the day. Take a moment to center yourself mentally, and visualize that you're standing on a huge shower of white light. Imagine that you are standing in a large bottle-shaped cylinder and you are filling the cylinder with this beautiful, soothing shower of divine light. It fills the entire vessel and upwards to twelve feet above and around you. On the bottom of your feet, you can visualize little valves that you will open to allow negativity and stress to leave through to the earth, while at the same time you are filling up your energy and physical body with this shower of divine light. This light contains the protection of unconditional love. You will feel that unconditional love from your own God-Self. If you choose, you may also invite the energy of your special Archangel or ascended master over to light you and transmit their healing energy as well. You can do this for anywhere from one to three minutes depending on how much time you have.

Now when you are in the presence of someone challenging, turn on the unconditional love from your heart like you would a gas stove, and feel this love not only for you, but for the person you are interacting with. Having the presence of your God-Self or other beloved spiritual being will help you feel protected, safe and loved from within. Nothing is more protective than unconditional love for humanity, one human at a time.

Do this exercise as often as you like. Over the long term, it will have tremendous healing benefits.

Part III

Health and Healing

125

Chapter 14

Understanding Your Health

Your health is connected to everything you have learned thus far. Your illnesses, accidents, everyday cuts, bumps and bruises are not as random as you would think. Every single physical problem has its cause rooted in your emotional or mental state, or connects to issues surrounding your karma and life lessons for this life. Even accidents are reflective of our emotional attitude and mental state, though they seem random and accidental. How you view your life – positive or negative – affects your well-being. Is your glass half full or half empty? Do you blame others for making you feel sick, or bad emotionally? Do you blame others for your accidents? From outer appearances, it seems like an accident has been caused by you or another individual randomly. I'm going to tell you that everything that happens to you – physically, emotionally, mentally, or accidentally – you *attracted* to yourself. And I mean everything. This is a hard concept to realize, accept and learn from. But, as you ponder this concept and really examine past situations in your life, like what was going on emotionally when you got injured; or what you were constantly thinking about when you became ill, you will begin to feel this statement is correct.

The good news is that once you do accept this fact, it can be very empowering because now you can begin the process of taking responsibility for your health on all levels. Begin by asking questions to yourself: Why did this so upset me? Why do I keep having small accidents? Why do I keep catching colds and flus so easily? What's wrong with my stomach? Why do I have headaches, allergies, joint pain, chronic ear infections, sinusitis, etc.? You get the picture.

The obvious cause may seem like it's your diet, catching

someone else's germs, pollen during spring or fall. If we blame our diets exclusively, then wouldn't everyone get the same illness doing the same things? Someone can smoke cigarettes their whole life and never get lung cancer, emphysema, or other lung diseases. Another person can get lung cancer without ever having smoked, or been in a smoking environment. What is the difference between these two people? Their divine blueprint created patterns and life lessons that created different health problems. That's not to say that you should go out and begin smoking. Smoking causes a whole host of health problems in all parts of the body not just the lungs. Negative external factors like poor diet, smoking, drinking, doing drugs, can exaggerate physical tendencies towards certain illnesses or diseases. If your immune system is strong because your emotional state is strong and you have a confident and positive mental attitude, you won't catch the flu, colds, ear infections or any other immune-related illness. Think about it. If you or someone you know and love has a poor diet, what might be the reason why they keep eating the wrong foods. Well, intellectually you can say, maybe they don't know better. That might be partially true. But emotionally, it could reveal a pattern of self-destructive behavior, or a pattern of feeling that they don't deserve to have good health because they don't feel they deserve love or good things to happen to them. They could even be replacing the love they don't feel they have with food. Addictive eating behaviors could also indicate past-life trauma or residual negative patterns. Eating foods that support our health can have a positive effect emotionally and mentally as well.

If you scanned the Table of Contents of this book, you can see that an entire section of this book has been devoted to the issue of health and healing. The quality of our life and ease at which we experience life will be greatly improved when we heal what's ailing us. There are many different ways to address healing naturally. Take a moment at this point of the book to re-read the chapter on chakras. This will be the beginning of understanding the areas of the body as they relate to physical illnesses and diseases and their connection to the emotions and mental attitude surrounding a chakra. There can be exceptions to certain illnesses and this usually relates to an unusual past-life event that is so unique that once the cause is known through past-life regression, it can be healed quickly.

Using myself as an example, as a child I had a lot of chronic illnesses. When I was very young, I had frequent and painful ear infections. Later on, in elementary school, I suffered regularly with asthma which could keep me out of school for a week at a time. My immune system was always compromised and throughout my youth, teen years and twenties, I suffered numerous sore throats, colds, and food allergies appeared when I hit my late twenties with terrible physical reactions. In my twenties, I also suffered issues surrounding my digestive system. You can see there was a negative emotional pattern that connected to my immune system. Like most people, I would go to the doctor for medical intervention and get medicine for my asthma, allergies, and antibiotics for my various infections. As you may have experienced already, these do not usually heal the problem – at least not permanently anyway. It wasn't until my late thirties when I began learning about alternative and natural healing modalities that I started to witness my various health problems go away. And not only did my *physical* healing improve, but while working with natural healing modalities like Reiki, holistic chiropractic care, essential oils, etc., my mental and emotional connections began to heal as well. I'm 50 years old and I'm in better health now than I was in my teens, twenties and thirties. The only pills I pop into my mouth are multi-vitamins and natural supplements.

Let's look at the definition and meaning of the word: holistic or holism.

Holism: 1. The view that a whole system of beliefs must be analyzed rather than simply its individual components. 2. The theory of the importance of taking all of somebody's physical, mental and social conditions into account in the treatment of illness.

In other words holism treats the whole person not just a set of symptoms or external causes (i.e. there's a flu bug going around.) Interestingly enough, when you choose to heal something holistically, it doesn't matter what natural means you use, once you start using it, it automatically begins healing you on every level – even if you aren't aware of it. For instance, going back to me and my garden variety of health issues, I began by introducing two natural means for healing my illnesses – essential oils and improved diet. Just by changing my diet gradually and using essential oils to heal my everyday illnesses caused my body to begin to fix itself, not just temporarily – the process had begun to heal these problems permanently. This went slowly, but the process was started. In changing my diet, I also began detoxifying my body through natural supplements, as well as healthier food choices.

It's important to know that when you begin the process of healing yourself, a lot of detoxifying goes on even if you are not specifically choosing to detoxify your body. What is being detoxified are old negative emotional patterns that could come from your childhood, past lives or even current patterns that formed when you began elementary school to now. When an emotion is being detoxified, it often results in re-experiencing that emotion as it is preparing to leave your body. Almost always, nothing is released that you are not ready to release so usually you will not have to deal with anything you aren't ready to deal with. You are young though and many, many things that will be offered in this book will improve the quality of your life. You are more fortunate than me in that you have chosen a spiritual path at a wonderfully early age. I began learning these things at a much later age – when I was nearly 40.

In this section, one chapter will briefly highlight some natural healing methods that would work wonders for your young bodies. Anything that is included in this book would be safe for all ages. Also included will also be things you can do for yourself that require no money. The trick here is to constantly be aware of every sensation you feel in your body at any given time. This is in keeping with using your intuition which we discussed in Part I. If something doesn't feel right in your body, then you shouldn't do it. Although everything I will be offering in this book is safe and beneficial for everyone, not everything works for everyone. If you begin using essential oils, some oils will work better with your chemistry than others. Music healing might resonate more with you than verbal affirmations for improving your emotional state. Use your intuition along with your mental knowledge. Always, always, check in by tuning in.

Also included in this section are ways to deal with your external world – from negative people, situations and vibrations, to a healing means in dealing with difficult relationships; ways to protect yourself from others; the power of words – both others' and your own; and the tremendous benefits of music and the many ways you can utilize it for healing.

Chapter 15

You Are What You Eat

What you put into your body for daily nourishment, energy and sustenance is the single most important choice you can make towards creating excellent health. Whether you are the age of 13 reading this, or 23, you have a lot of control over what you put into your body. If you are filling it with processed foods, sugar, salt, prescriptions medicines, you may already be feeling the negative effects of these items in the form of chronic health conditions, brain fog or low energy, acne or poor skin appearance, frequent stomach problems, like constipation or acid indigestion, headaches, frequent colds...you get the picture. This chapter will focus on the basics of good nutrition and eating. When my children or I get sick, the first thing I do is turn to look at what they have been eating. I then use better food choices to assist in healing them and myself.

You can learn now how and what to eat based on how it makes your body feel. If you are already eating pretty well, that's excellent. Perhaps you just need to tweak some things. If not, then it is my hope that this information will be helpful and valuable to you as you begin to make changes in your diet. As you read this section, you will see that the longest chapter will be on food; because a healthy diet is the foundation of good health, and good health creates the environment to develop spiritually. Let's begin.

Water

Water is the singularly most important item to put into your body. Most of us do not drink enough pure water, myself included (though I try). Water helps remove toxins, improves energy levels, mental focus and concentration. It improves our blood flow and circulation. It assists in keeping your heart healthy because when you are dehydrated your heart is working harder. It assists in keeping your digestion moving properly thus preventing cramps, intestinal agitation and/or constipation. It keeps your kidneys running without being strained. It pretty much improves all organ functions in your body when we drink enough pure water. It can lower a fever. It improves our skin, preventing acne and wrinkles, and adds overall vitality to our appearance. The best formula for determining how much water you need for your body is to take your body weight and visualize it in ounces. For instance, if you weigh 100 pounds, and you convert that to 100 ounces (100 / 8 ounces = 12.5 glasses a day of water). This is easier than it looks. Most tall drinking glasses hold anywhere from twelve to sixteen ounces. So, using that 100 pounds of weight and dividing it by twelve ounces, you should have eight 12-oz bottles or glasses of water a day. You will notice within a few days of regularly doing this how much better you are feeling. If you are overweight, it will help fill you so you begin to eat less. It will also improve your energy level and your mental focus.

Vegetables

I separated vegetables from fruits as they serve our body in different ways. Many vegetables contain a perfect combination of protein, fiber, vitamins and minerals such as all the vegetables in the bean family. Different vegetables address health in different parts and organs of the body. Here is a list of common highly nutritious vegetables that all of us should have on a regular basis. Without burdening you with too many vegetables that you may not even like, I focused in on those that most people do like.

Potatoes: Not in the form of French fries, potato chips or mashed potatoes and gravy, but they can be baked, roasted, put in soup and stews where they have tremendous healthful value. Potatoes are a very balanced vegetable. You could survive on potatoes if you were on a deserted island far more than many other vegetables. It is always preferable to purchase them in organic form. Since they are a root vegetable, traditional farming practices that use pesticides will leave chemical residues in the soil. This would unfortunately be utilized by the growing potatoes. So, always try to purchase organic potatoes.

Carrots: Are extremely versatile. They can be steamed, roasted, eaten raw, put in soup, or healthy coleslaw. They are high in beta-carotene and a host of other beneficial vitamins and minerals. They are also a starchy and fiber-filled vegetable which have tremendous benefits to your digestive system. If you are trying to lose weight, the fiber in carrots will help you to feel fuller. They are also soothing to an upset stomach when liquified through a juicer. Again, this is another food that should be purchased in organic form.

Leafy Vegetables: These are usually eaten raw in salads. Spinach has some versatility and can be added to baked macaroni and cheese, mashed potatoes, soups and stews without creating any backlash of poor taste. Leafy vegetables, in addition to fiber, also contain natural forms of sulfur, silicon, and salts that deliver balanced nutrition when eaten in their natural form and not processed. These three "s" compounds have amazing benefits to our nervous system, and the chemicals in our brain. One should have a salad every day. If you find a dressing you like, then have them with that, but don't drown your salad in it otherwise you will cancel out the lettuce's benefits. Try out different lettuces – some are bitter, some are milder. All are good for your body.

Beans: Are an excellent source of protein and fiber. If you are a vegetarian, then chances are beans are a regular part of your diet.

If not, then they should be. There are so many varieties of beans that you can sample and try to figure out which ones you like. You can add them to rice, soup, bake them, have them as a side dish, put them in salad, eat them dried. Try not to choose refried beans because, again, they are overly processed. You want to get the nutritional benefits from beans.

Broccoli and Cauliflower: These vegetables often get a bad rap for not being kid-friendly in regards to taste. But, they are also very versatile in the many ways you can incorporate them in your meals. Broccoli can be added to a traditional tomato sauce. Cauliflower can be roasted with a nut or olive oil and salt. They can be used in soup and pureed for a creamy soup texture. They are great with a variety of sauces and ethnic dishes like Indian and Thai foods. Give them a try. They are good, fiber foods and good for the brain. Think about it; they kind of look like they have a brain shape.

Onions and Garlic: These are two different vegetables but are often used together or have the same purpose. Onions and garlic have tremendous healing benefits when we catch a cold or flu or any bacterial or viral condition that affects our immune system. They too, like the leafy vegetables have a form of sulfur that gives them their odor but is beneficial to our bodies. They are excellent raw as well as cooked in our sauces, stews, roasted dishes etc. Try to include them in your diet and be sure to have them when you are sick.

Other, less popular, vegetables to try are: beets, celery, leeks, sweet potatoes, okra, cabbage, asparagus, Brussels sprouts and parsnips, to name a few. But, including the above list of veggies, is an excellent place to start if you are not already including them in your diet.

Fruits

Fruits are different in certain ways from vegetables as they are great detoxifiers for the body. They almost all create an alkaline ash in the body. This means that it removes the acid-forming residues from meat, processed carbohydrates such as pasta and bread, processed foods and sweets as well as toxins from prescription drugs and the environment. Having an alkaline body is a healthy body.

Here is something of note: acid foods (and drugs) create mucus in the body. Mucus creates inflammation and inflammation leads to disease. Eating a greater portion of alkaline foods than acid foods creates the balance in your body for optimal health.

Fruits clean out your body in sweet and delicious ways, while also providing a perfect balance of vitamins, minerals, enzymes and fiber. Please note that there are several fruits that people normally serve as a vegetable, such as cucumbers and tomatoes, but technically they are a fruit with all their fruit benefits. Here's a top-line list of excellent fruits that should be included in your diet regularly.

Apples: Apples are one of the most nutritious foods from nature. It is true what they say, "an apple a day keeps the doctor away." Apples, like onions, contain a lot of compounds that prevent illness and disease. There is such a tremendous variety of apples to choose from. Sour, tart, sweet, yellow, red, green, pink – there should be at least one variety that you can enjoy. Please note that eating apple pie is not giving you a serving of apples. To get the best benefit from apples, eat them raw. This is a fruit that you should always eat organic.

Bananas: Although it's not a traditional fruit with seeds as with many of the fruits that are listed, it's an extremely healthful food. It's one of the most balanced foods nutritionally that you can add to your diet. It has fiber, potassium and a host of other compounds, vitamins and minerals. You should consider having a banana every day. It's also a good food for weight loss.

Berries – including strawberries, blueberries, blackberries, and raspberries: I've clumped these together to save space. These fruits all contain a tremendous amount of anti-oxidants and vitamin C. Each of these berries contains compounds unique to them including those compounds that give them their vibrant color. Individually they have a varied number of health benefits to our bodies. They not only assist in keeping our bodies alkaline, they are excellent for heart health and keeping our hormonal systems in balance. It is preferable to have these organic as well, as traditional farming has them covered in excessive amounts of pesticides.

Oranges: Oranges fresh-squeezed and raw, or eaten whole are extremely healthful; much more so than buying a bottle of orange juice in the store. Oranges are good for overall immune-system health, and vitamin C has been found, in high amounts, to relieve pain in the body from various other ailments. Many of the fruits I've listed already contain high levels of vitamin C. So, in addition to your vitamin-C supplement, eat a lot of fruit when you are sick. If you ate just fruit and drank water when you were ill, your body would recover soooo much sooner than if you eat a regular diet during an illness.

Lemons: Okay, eating a raw lemon is not exactly enticing, but adding lemon juice to your glass of water is, and lemons are up there when it comes to alkalizing foods. It is excellent for your liver health, and since the liver cleans our blood, we definitely want to have a healthy liver. You can juice raw lemons with sweeter-tasting fruits like apples or oranges and get the benefits that way. It is often added to fish and sauces as well.

Grapes: Most people love grapes – red or green. Grapes are really good at cleaning out bacteria and mucus from the body. They are sugary tasting, but in their raw form our bodies receive a perfect balance of natural grape compounds that is good for our heart health. This is another fruit that should be eaten raw and not from a bottle.

The Melons (Watermelon, Cantaloupe, Honeydew): All are high in vitamin C, water content for replacing waters and sugars in our bodies, and fiber. It's also a highly alkalizing food for improving our total health.

Cucumbers: The water content in cucumbers really cleans out our bodies, improving our digestion, thus reducing inflammation. They are a cooling food and can be eaten when trying to reduce a fever in combination with other natural means such as drinking plenty of water and putting peppermint essential oil on your feet. They too contain natural salts and minerals to replenish our bodies after physical activities or excessive perspiring.

There are many other fruits, such as pears, pomegranates, grapefruits, kiwi fruit, and more, but this gives you an excellent overview of popular and tasty fruits that should be included in your diet every week.

Nuts and Seeds

Nuts and seeds are highly nutritious and an excellent source of protein and fiber. If you have a nut allergy, chances are there are some seed varieties you can eat as a substitute and vice-versa. If you do not have an allergy to peanuts, tree nuts, sesame seeds, sunflower seeds, then you will definitely want to include these in your diet.

Walnuts and Almonds: Are two of the most highly nutritious nuts you can eat. Raw is always better, but if you bake them in granola, or roast them plain, you will also receive tremendous benefits. They provide a highly nutritious form of proteins and healthy fats. As a matter of fact, even though they contain fat, it is an extremely beneficial form of fat and can help in the process of losing weight for improving your health. Walnuts contain high levels of omega-3 fatty acids which are great for your brain. (They even look like your brain when you remove the shell.) Almonds are an excellent source of calcium. Calcium is not just good for your bones and teeth, but it is also a very calming mineral to have in your body.

Other nuts including Brazil nuts, pecans, pistachios and cashews are also good for your health. Cashews and Brazil nuts contain a good source of magnesium which is important for your nervous system. Peanuts too are healthful even though they are part of the bean family.

If you prefer eating your nuts as nut butter, it is better to purchase it raw so you get all the nut oils and fiber for proper health. Buying Skippy or Jif is not the same thing. With the other processed, manmade ingredients contained in those brands, you are harming your body instead.

Pumpkin Seeds: These are one of the most highly nutritious seeds you can eat. They are also high in zinc, magnesium, manganese, as well as protein and fiber. Pumpkin seeds also contain a wide variety of vitamin-E forms within the complexity of the seed. Raw is better, but lightly toasted, roasted (no more than 15-20 minutes), or baked in granola is still very good.

Sunflower Seeds: Are very high in vitamin E as well as containing compounds that have an anti-inflammatory effect. They are also a good source of magnesium, selenium, and vitamins B1, B3 and B6. They also have benefits of neutralizing the effects of free radicals on our body's cells. You can eat them raw or roasted, or in granola, cereal, oatmeal, salads.

Sesame Seeds: Are very high in copper which is naturally anti-inflammatory. Eating them also reduces your cholesterol which is increasingly becoming a concern for teens and young adults. It's not just an old people's disease anymore. The seeds are also a good source of calcium, manganese, and magnesium. They are so tasty that you can sprinkle them on to many foods, including salads, pastas, or anything Thai or Chinese.

Super Foods

Now, I want to include a special group of foods that bear the "super" title. There are supermodels, superstars, superheroes. Well, there are also super foods. These are foods that are highly beneficial to our bodies for a variety of reasons. They may grow in certain regions of the world where the soil, natural environment and water sources contain high levels of nutrients. These foods also have qualities that allow you to use them in a variety of ways...not just for eating. The following foods fit this profile.

Chia Seeds: These tiny little black seeds shaped like tiny balls pack quite a lot of nutrition. They are high in calcium, omega-3s, protein, fiber, potassium. They have a unique quality to them when they get to the stomach. As the seeds begin to break down, they get gooey and slimy. This quality gives them the ability to pull out toxins and residue from bodies as they go through our digestive tract...leaving it cleaner than when they entered. In terms of taste, when you add them to your food, they don't really have a specific flavor or taste, so it's possible to add them to just about any meal such as tomato sauce, macaroni and cheese, salads, breads, stews, dipping sauces, and whatever else you can think of. You only need one tablespoon a day to satisfy a full serving of chia seeds.

Coconut Oil: This tasty oil is extremely healthy and versatile. There are entire books on the health benefits of coconut oil. The reason is because of the type of fats it contains. These are called **m**edium **c**hain **f**atty **a**cids (a.k.a, MCFAs). MCFAs are excellent for good heart health, weight loss, cancer and diabetes prevention, strengthen our immune systems and have amazing beauty benefits to our hair and skin. And that's just the tip of the iceberg. You can swirl coconut oil in your mouth to rid your teeth and gums of cavity-causing bacteria. This is called oil pulling. The MCFAs are also highly beneficial for growth and development. As this book is written for teens and young adults, this means *your* growth and development. They key ingredient in MCFAs is the lauric acid. It is naturally produced in a mother's breast milk which is highly nutritious for babies who are breastfed as it's highly anti-microbial properties strengthen the immune system of the child. Coconut oil's MCFAs contain the highest levels of lauric acid, making coconut oil extremely healthful for the rest of the non-breastfeeding population. You can often substitute olive oil or vegetable oil with coconut oil in recipes. I use coconut oil all the time when I bake cookies, brownies, cakes, granola. It will not overpower your baked goods with coconut flavor, but it will make it more nutritious and less detrimental to your health than other fats and oils.

Raw Apple Cider Vinegar: This vinegar has tremendous health benefits both inside the body and out. It's great for detoxifying your body – removing the "sludge" from your organs, cells and generally your entire insides. It also makes a great skin toner. It balances your skin – making it neither dry nor oily. It has amazing benefits for your entire digestive tract. To receive the full benefits of this food, you must consume it raw. If it isn't raw, then it is unable to deliver the ka-pow you want for your body.

Black Cumin Seeds and the Oil: These seeds and the oil they are made from are highly nutritious. There are a couple of areas in the Mideast, Northern Africa and parts of Asia like India, from which black cumin seeds come from. But, the black cumin that comes from Egypt has the highest therapeutic value. It's healing benefits those who suffer from asthma, allergies, immune disorders, colds, flus, toothaches, headaches and it's amazing with skin disorders of any kind. High quality, Egyptian black cumin seed can be purchased on line from ethical suppliers. It's a food or supplement that's worth considering for your health. In terms of how to use it in your meals, the seeds are usually ground so you can sprinkle it on your salads, dipping sauces, stews, soups. The taste is milder than regular cumin. I like to bake my potato French fries instead of frying them. I sprinkle ground black cumin seeds on them along with Himalayan sea salt and ground black pepper. It's so simple and so tasty. I use the oil in homemade lotions and healing ointments as it's amazing for healing various skin conditions.

Papaya: Is a more amazing fruit than one would realize. It too has received recognition with books published about its myriad of health benefits. Papaya is as sweet as a cantaloupe or honeydew, but denser. It grows in places like Hawaii, Central America and Mexico – in hot and tropical climates. It's an amazing detoxifying food than excels in normalizing the PH balance in our stomachs and digestive tracts. The enzyme papain, which is contained in the papaya has been made into supplements for relieving stomach problems. It's also been made into an excellent healing salve for skin irritations, cuts and rashes. It is very high in vitamin C, calcium and fiber. Its health benefits also include immune healing properties, improving heart health, anti-inflammatory benefits, and skin health. If your body feels the burden from eating too many processed or heavy foods, eat this fruit in abundance and you will begin to feel much better. To eat, simply wash the fruit, slice, peel, scoop out the seeds and cut into chunks for eating. (The seeds are highly nutritious too, but I admit they don't taste great.)

Green Tea: I couldn't forget the green tea. Green tea has a compound in it called 'catechins.' It has excellent benefits for brain health. It lowers blood pressure and cholesterol, has heart health benefits, improves the immune system, and helps lower weight to name a few of the benefits. Have it hot or cold with a little honey or agave nectar and a little lemon (helps us to absorb the catechins better) and you are good to go. Having green tea daily is an excellent addition to your diet. There are other super foods but these are a start as you make changes to your diet.

The Rest of the Food on Your Plate

As you can see, the focus of this chapter has been on truly the most important foods you need to include in your diet. It should go without saying that in regards to the other food groups, here's the rule of thumb you should consider for optimal health:

Starches and Carbohydrates: It is preferable to not have highly processed breads and baked goods. A little pasta with your Italian meal is fine. A lot of pasta many times a week with heavy sauces that include meat, cream or cheese is not. When choosing bread, whole grain (not whole wheat or white), is much healthier. There are a variety of "new" breads that are made with grains other than wheat – particularly for people who are gluten intolerant. You don't need to be gluten intolerant to enjoy gluten-free breads though. Wheat sensitivities can include fatigue, fogginess and even bloating after eating a meal with processed wheat products. If you feel this happens to you, consider removing some of the wheat in your diet. You'd be surprised how much better you feel.

Meat/Poultry/Fish: A little goes a long way, and always choose all-natural or organic meats that aren't filled with antibiotics and unnatural feed. Read the labels on packages of meat, and don't let your parents be seduced by the meat sales or cheap prices. You are paying more than you realize with your health. If you are a meat eater, the amount of meat on your plate should be no larger than your fist. Use this as a good rule of thumb and you won't overdo the heavy animal protein.

Dairy: Again, extreme moderation is preferable. There are healthy choices, and not so healthy. Your cow milk should ALWAYS be organic. Cows in traditional dairy farms are always getting sick because of poor living conditions, and that can seep into their milk. So, stick with organic milk. Also, always choose real butter, not margarine. It's been proven that good-quality butter helps raise the good cholesterol. Good cholesterol keeps your blood vessel walls flexible so they don't harden and create blockages. High-quality cheeses such as goat cheese or sheep's milk cheese are a very good option. That being said, you do not need dairy in your diet for calcium or vitamin D. You can obtain calcium from an enormous variety of fruits and vegetables and vitamin D you can get directly from the sun, or through high-quality supplements in the dark winter months where getting out into the sun is not a possibility.

Sweets/Sugar: As with all the other categories, very little goes a long way. Many of us have sweet tooth or consider ourselves "chocoholics." There's nothing wrong with indulging in sweet treats as long as they are not full of high fructose corn syrup and the many, many unnatural, factory-made chemicals you find in traditional package brands. Stay away from anything with high fructose corn syrup, hydrogenated oils, propylene glycol, artificial colors, flavors and preservatives, and stick with products that have ingredients you recognize as using when you bake at home. If you can purchase it, then learn to make it. You'd be surprised that what you can make tastes better than the store-bought version. More and more good science is showing evidence on how these manmade chemicals are harming our brains, and bodies. Eliminating them from your diet will have a huge positive impact on your health. In a nutshell, your plate should consist of more than 50% veggies and fruit, and the rest your protein and carbohydrates.

Transitioning can be hard, but it can be done gradually and slowly. Start off by food-shopping with your mother or father, and begin reading ingredient labels. Educating yourself on what is in your food is really the first step. Over the last fourteen years I have read a tremendous number of books, and have done extensive research on the subject of eating and nutrition. I've applied what I learned with my family, and shared the knowledge with the clients who come to see me for healing. This chapter is a just a basic introduction to explain how you can eat healthy food as a source of healing to your body. Do your own research after reading this book.

Chapter 16

Energy: Understanding the Power of Words and Thoughts

Positive, strongly felt thoughts and inner talk will generate positive outcomes and experiences in so many different ways.

The powerful and important concept you will learn in this chapter is simply this: Thoughts are things; every single thought creates an energy. Remember in elementary school you learned what a noun is; it's a person, place or thing. Well, if you use the word "thought" in a sentence, your school teacher would identify that word as a noun. Why? Because thoughts are things. Yes, yes, it's also a verb – but thinking creates thoughts. There are all kinds of thoughts we run in our heads, happy thoughts, memory replay, negative self-talk, neutral thoughts, negative thought patterns, wishful thoughts, dreamy thoughts, negative projections of what's happening around us. Truly there are quite a wide variety of thoughts that run through our minds each day. So what do *you* think about all the time? Take a few moments to think about what it is you actually think about or say to yourself. Is it all negative chatter? Are there negative loops running around in circles in your head that you constantly say about yourself? Do you project negative outcomes on situations? Do you say negative thoughts to yourself about others – even people you love and care about because they annoyed you? Do you run a constant computer feed of negative self-talk about yourself that makes you feel bad all the time? Or do you have positive thoughts and believe the best of people and situations at all times? For example, on the morning of a school test or exam, do you think, "Oh, I'll ace this" and "I'm going to do really well on this test." Or does your mind say, "I just know I'm going to fail. I don't know anything" or "Tests make me too nervous to do well."

If you have a continual and constant pattern of more negative thoughts than positive, then your everyday world will seem sad, disappointing, frustrating, and generally depressing on some level. You won't be able to be happy very much even when something good happens because, you'll have spent so much time on the negative, you will even find fault with the good things that happen in your favor.

I'm here to tell you that changing your thoughts and the emotions that go with them are one of the few things in life that you have complete control over. You can't control change. You can't control people. You can't control your environment externally. But, you *can* control your thoughts. Interestingly enough, when you control your thoughts in a positive way, all of the above will change anyway in the end. You've heard the saying that you can't change people. You have to accept them as they are. But try as we might, many of us still try to change others. Parents think they can change their children. Well, they can teach you manners, social behaviors and such, but they cannot inherently change the basic nature of their children. Have you felt like your parents have tried to change you? Be reassured that even though they are misguided in that effort, they did it out of love; not realizing that it was futile and it made you feel bad about yourself.

When we focus on the only person we can change, ourselves, everyone around us will *seem* to have changed too because our perceptions will have shifted. Relationships will improve. Events will run better; challenging situations will improve, and your overall outlook on life will be better because your positive thoughts helped to make you feel better emotionally. It all starts with you. Will everything go perfectly? No, there are too many variables in the form of other people who have Free Will like you. But, will life be happier and more enjoyable? Yes, it will. Will you feel less overwhelmed by the challenges you face academically, socially, physically, within your family, etc.? Yes, absolutely you will.

At first, beginning the conscious, deliberate process of changing your thought patterns will be difficult as you need to become vigilant and persistent in making the effort to think about what it is you think about. I reiterate thoughts are energy; thoughts are things. Neutral thoughts such as "I need to buy more toothpaste today," or "I have to mail out a birthday card" are fine. Thinking, "Oh, I hate going shopping for birthday cards because it takes so much time" is not helpful in creating positive outcomes.

When you wake up in the morning, what are your first thoughts? Try to be conscious of them, as they can set the tone for your whole day. Try a positive affirmation upon waking in the morning like, "This is going to be such an amazing day – wonderful surprises are in store and I look forward to experiencing them." A wonderful surprise could be that your social studies class is covering a unit on your favorite period of history that day. Your friend tells you that you look great in that color. You discover a helpful solution to a problem you've been trying to solve. Appreciating and recognizing the little things of our everyday lives is what gives us such a joyful, happy and peaceful feeling. Positive thoughts create positive feelings. Positive feelings transform people into positive human beings. Positive human beings attract more positive experiences, people, friendships and outcomes into their world.

Gratitude is one of the biggest generators of positivity out there. It's the single most important way to raise your vibrations and elevate you spiritually. Gratitude by its very nature helps you focus on the positive parts of your life and world exclusively. You would be unable to be grateful in a negative way because that's not how gratitude works. In Chapter 1 there was a little discussion about gratitude. To go a little deeper on this subject, I'd like to tell you of a way to create feelings of gratitude every day, and it is this. Purchase a small, little notebook and call it your "gratitude journal." Each day, take a moment to write as little as a sentence or two, or as much as a page about one thing you are grateful for that day, or that moment. You could write about people in your life, situations that worked out, talents you possess, the good grade you got in school, something that worked out in your favor, the cool gift you received, whatever comes to mind that you are grateful for. Include with your gratitude a thank you to that person on paper. The energy of that thank you will reach them and raise their vibrations as much as raising yours in writing it. Keep this journal separate from your regular journal. I'll explain why in a moment. As I mentioned in Chapter 1, gratitude can raise your vibrations and energy more than any other form of positive activity. Being grateful to God, your angels, ascended masters, spirit guides and other special spiritual beings has a tremendous uplifting feeling to your entire body and energy system. Don't forget to show your appreciation to them each and every day in the form of prayers, decrees or affirmations. You can also include them in your journal if you so choose. Now, the reason for keeping this journal separate is that when you are in a funk or bad mood, you can take a quiet moment and re-read what you are grateful for, and this will change how you are feeling at that moment. Doing this when you feel sad, depressed or just having what seems to be a bad day can totally shift your perspective again to a more positive outlook. Re-reading your grateful thoughts will also be healing, and will reposition the focus of your life on what's truly important instead of the little annoyances and disappointments that truly have no real meaning in your life.

So, yes, thoughts are things. Negative thought patterns can remain lodged in the cells of our body and our energy field. This is the cause of our illnesses. Some negative patterns we were born with as they are part of our past-life karma of which we have this life to correct and learn from. Some negative patterns became stuck from other people's negative thoughts about us. If we've had a lot of negative thoughts throughout our childhood, these thoughts will be lodged in our bodies as well. But the good news is, thoughts can be changed, and the negative memories in our bodies can be changed and removed. That's where healing comes in; we are in the driver seat of our own healing process. No one can heal us, but us. Oh, you can go to a medical doctor or a holistic healer to help you, but ultimately it's your Free Will and inner thought process that allows your body to heal successfully and/or permanently from all that ails you. Admittedly, there are many processes that go on in our body on a subconscious level that we are all unaware of, but giving yourself permission to heal from something whether it's emotionally, psychologically or physically based will make all the difference in getting rid of these negative patterns that make us ill or feel bad even if you consciously didn't know what it was. In the second part of this chapter, I will provide some tools for protecting yourself from known and unknown external negative energy.

Scientifically speaking, every human being generates electro-magnetic waves around their body. Your body's electromagnetic signature is unique to you. If you visit a friend and sit on their chair or couch for a couple of hours while visiting, your energy remains there for a time. If you are a really sensitive person, you can pick up on someone else's energetic residue when you sit in a public place. It's also in the very air you breathe. Have you ever gone into an elevator and felt strange, or stagnant vibes or energies that make you feel low or sad? Next time you sit in a movie theatre or restaurant, tune in to the vibes you pick up from where you choose to sit. If you feel more negative than positive, change your seat.

Yes, changing your thoughts is a process and if you've gotten into a bad habit of negative self-talk over many years, then it's going to take practice and diligence to constantly check in to your thoughts to see what you're thinking about all the time. You might find it amusing to know that my thoughts are accompanied by a music soundtrack. I always, always, have music in my head. Some of the time, it's not of my conscious choosing, so I pay attention to what's playing because sometimes there's a message I need to hear. Most times, it's reflective of what's going on in my life at the moment, or on that day. I highly recommend asking your spirit guides and teachers to help you program some very nice music in your brain. It's most helpful in keeping you conscious of your thoughts. The last chapter in this section will focus entirely on using music for healing.

Negative Talk – Both Inner and Out – About Other People

In addition to changing your inner chatter and negative self-talk, it's also very important to stop having negative thoughts and words about others as well. This includes gossiping. To get into a habit of not talking negatively about people is one of the hardest changes we can make. But it's extremely important in improving the quality of your daily life. It's important to know that all discordant thoughts you generate about others comes right back to you like a boomerang.

Okay, here's a scenario. You go to your school or college class in the morning. You run into a friend, and she wants to tell you about what happened to Amy yesterday. You listen and it's full of information of which your friend has plenty of opinions about. Amy said this, and isn't she just stupid, or silly or crazy. You have a few choices: replying in kind and making your own judgmental comments; smile uncomfortably and refrain from adding any comments; say something positive in Amy's favor; or reply that you would rather not talk about Amy as you have no opinion about what she did. This is a tough one and there are no black and white answers for every situation. One thing is for sure, adding more negative and judgmental comments definitely is *not* the way to go. Many times being silent is your best option because then you don't need to engage further in this topic, and you can introduce a new topic of conversation. At the same time you can send healing or positive thoughts to the person who was spoken negatively about. If someone talks badly about you, that negative energy gets to you even if you don't directly or consciously feel it. By the same token, when you send negative words or thoughts to someone, you hurt them as well as yourself.

Consider it a relief to have no opinions about anyone. Because then you don't need to drain your mental focus or energy on people or situations that have nothing to do with you or your life. This is what is called detachment. That doesn't mean you don't care about your friends and acquaintances, but being detached means you don't need to carry their burdens or emotional stuff as your own. Your goal is to be unconditionally loving and compassionate, not judgmental or opinionated. When I am personally in a situation where someone is speaking negatively about someone else, I either keep silent or mentally send unconditionally loving thoughts to both the person being talked about as well as the person doing the negative talking or I ask the individual to stop talking about him/her. And when I say these things, I stay in a mental place of not judging the person gossiping either. I am respectful of their own place in their journey of life. Each and every day, I keep choosing to stay neutral about all those around me, to sending more loving words and thoughts and to stop having negative opinions about others. And if I accidentally slip up (and I do), I forgive myself and send loving thoughts to the other person to correct my mistake.

It's like that old saying, "If you can't say something nice, then don't say anything." You can add, "If you can't think something nice, then don't think anything" too. What happens with all these negative thoughts flying around like soft, sticky balls is that they get permanently stuck to your energy field. Over time, these negative thoughts begin to penetrate us in hundreds of different ways and locations on your body. Here is another quote from *The Magic Presence* that illustrates this point.

"When one wishes to give way to his own feeling of resistance rather than still that feeling and replace it by Peace, he destroys himself – mind, body and world – because the Law is that whatever discordant thought and feeling is sent forth by a human being, it must first vibrate through the brain and body of the sender before it can reach into the rest of the Universe. After swinging out, it begins the return journey to its creator. While coming back, it gathers more of its kind, and that becomes the accretion of which the individual's world is composed. This is *The Law*, and it is Immutable. [*The Magic Presence, King Godfre Ray, Saint Germain Press, Pg. 117*]

Spiritual Protection

The best protection you can put on is by turning on your heart stream of unconditional love. Nothing negative can penetrate if you are in a constant state of unconditional love for everyone including animals and nature. That includes your parents, siblings, extended family, friends as well as the annoying store clerk, the stern teacher, the angry driver, the scary stranger, and your enemies. This is the hardest lesson and the hardest exercise of all – feeling unconditional love – that is true unconditional love for people you dislike or have harmed you in some way. I have seen and read stories of the power of unconditional love demonstrated in the most horrible situations with the most angry and scariest of people. True unconditional love not only heals, but it can also transform a person or situation for the better. There is a wonderful person who died in the 1980s whose life exemplifies this truth. Her name was Peace Pilgrim, and her book will be one of the recommended books that will be listed at the back of this book.

Don't feel bad if you are unable to generate that kind of feeling for people who have hurt you, injured you or made you angry. It's a process. Just being aware of this puts you on notice so that little by little you can change, as if you are adding beautiful gossamer layers of white healing silk over all of your four lower bodies. As you begin to make changes in your thoughts, verbal expression and emotional outlook, your aura and physical body will automatically begin to purify and clear itself.

Here are some things you can do to protect yourself:

1. Cross your arms across your midsection. Energy of all kinds enters through the third chakra – through the stomach and liver area. This is a minor way of protecting yourself from angry words during an argument or heated discussion. Another way is to simply turn your body away. If someone is upset, simply turn your body so you're not face-to-face with them and breathe.

2. Doing cleansing breaths also purifies you of any negative energy that may have entered your energy fields. With each in-breath, imagine that you are inhaling positive universal love, and when you exhale, imagine that you are releasing all the toxins of negative energies and purifying your body through the out-breath. Breathing has a lot of benefits. It detoxifies, purifies, calms and de-stresses us if we tune and focus on it.

3. Another tool is if you are trapped in an environment with someone who is upset, you can keep your mind in neutral by simply naming the objects in the room mentally. You are simply creating a mental diversion so you don't take on the emotions of the other individual or individuals who are actively unhappy.

4. Another simple exercise: As you dress for school visualize a protective white cylinder of light around you that remains with you all day protecting you. Keeping your

protective layer in the form of a cylinder allows you to receive spiritual love, healing and energy from above, while being protected from the external human world.

Indirect Negative Energy Attacks

Negative vibrations have a variety of ways of being absorbed by human beings. It doesn't always have to be a deliberate attack by others. Our energy fields and bodies can also be affected indirectly through various forms of media.

Watching violent movies and TV shows all the time can drain us energetically and we end up absorbing the feelings from the violence we are watching on the screen. It affects us. How many times did you watch a crime drama on TV or a violent movie and went home to bed thinking about what you watched. Did you sometimes have scary or bad dreams? You would have absorbed that negative energy. Try not to watch extremely violent films. They may seem exciting at the time, but they fill your bodies and minds with negative stuff that isn't always easy to shake off. Some violent movies can stay with us, and create fears based on whatever happened to the characters in the movie. Perhaps it created a new fear of something that you never thought of before, so now it's colored your perception, perhaps perma- nently. Yes, there are interesting dramas where bad things can happen to the characters, but if there's a good storyline where someone has learned a moral, lesson, had an epiphany about their life or situation, a relationship has improved, or their life improved because of their journey in the story, then yes, this would be different than watching violent crime or horror movies.

Other media that can be violent would be in the form of music, computer games, and violent sports like boxing. When you engage in these types of things, think about how they make you feel? Does it stir up anger in you? Do you feel defensive or hair trigger to overreact to something afterwards? If they always make you feel worse than before you started that activity, you might want to rethink what you are engaging in during your free time. Music that has violent or angry lyrics and harsh heavy metal guitars and drums will have a different affect than other types of music. This doesn't mean you shouldn't listen to rock music if you like it, but tune in to how any of your music makes you feel.

Computer games or game systems already can harm your health because of the electromagnetic frequencies they give off which can be harmful to our bodies over prolonged periods of time. But, if you are also playing violent, shoot-em-up types of games with graphic images, these are really detrimental to your mental, emotional and physical well-being. There's nothing positive about playing them, and you should consider not playing them anymore if you do.

Violent sports like boxing, wrestling and anything where the goal is to beat the heck out of someone is definitely not going to help your body feel good and positive. It will attract and draw out those issues you carry in you that make you angry, frustrated, impatient and stressed. All of these emotions are detrimental to our health.

Bottom line here is to be careful what kind of entertainment you seek. If you make a conscious effort to make different choices in movies, music and such, you will also add to the level of positive consciousness you are trying to create in your life. It all accumulates, so wouldn't you rather accumulate a momentum of good-feeling energy instead of depressingly angry energy. This affects all parts of your life. What you think about becomes your reality. Try not to fill it with images and thoughts gotten from violent and angry movies, music, sports and games.

Chapter 17

How To Learn From
Difficult Relationships and Situations

In this life, we have to deal with many, many different kinds of people and situations. It's all part of our lives for a reason. But, it doesn't mean we always know how to deal with it, so I'd like to devote a chapter on just this subject.

As has been discussed in previous chapters, there are life lessons we have programmed into our divine blueprint in order to learn lessons, heal karmic issues, or pay back karmic debt. Many of us in planning our current lives included a lot of karmic issues to heal in our divine plan in order to accelerate our spiritual growth. Having a lot of karmic lessons as you go through your life can be overwhelming and can possibly derail your success in overcoming it. Or worse, can cause you to create new karma. The biggest karmic lessons come in the form of people and relationships. These karmic relationships can happen between you and your parents, siblings, other family members, friends, teachers, neighbors, and acquaintances.

So I invite you to take a moment, and evaluate on paper (in your journal) all the people that you have had difficulty with – from immediate family members to acquaintances. Do you constantly have friction between you and your mother or father? Do you and your brother argue constantly – even more than you think you should as siblings? Did you ever have to work on a project with someone that really irritated you? Did you ever have a teacher where you always seemed to get on their bad side? How about that annoying neighbor, the classmate that stirs up trouble or makes fun of everyone? Now, take a second moment, and think about how you handled yourself in each and every situation. Did you get defensive? Are *you* the first to attack? Do you behave like a victim? Do you avoid the individual? Do you always think the worst and expect the worst from that person even before they do anything?

These are all little karmic life lessons coming into your life in many, many different ways. Some people will be with you for your whole life – like family members. Others will be in your life for a specific period of time. In each and every personal situation, you are both teacher and student. Sometimes the individual you are having difficulty with is the student and you are the teacher – and age makes no difference. Many adults can learn from children and life it supposed to work that way. We can benefit from these situations if we choose to. Some situations or relationships will be very hard to repair or heal, and some will be easier. It all depends on what the lesson is – and which person is the teacher or student in a given scenario.

Now, how do we handle these relationships? It would be great if all of us arrived with instruction packets on how to handle us from infancy to childhood to adulthood. But we don't. And if we did, where would the challenge be if we had all the answers in advance. Earth is a school, and humans are all students of the earth school. Progressing spiritually is like moving up a grade in school. Each lifetime where we live honorably, with love, and heal/learn our life lessons without incurring more karma will allow us to be born in the next life with more harmony and lesson difficulties – thus affording us more and more opportunities to advance spiritually until we graduate. This is Ascension and it should be the goal of every human being.

Since many of you that are reading this probably still live at home, let's methodically discuss the different types of relationships you might have in this stage of your life.

Parents: If you have a difficult relationship with one or both of your parents, this is a big karmic life lesson because chances are they will be in your life for a very long time. Healing this relationship will be huge for you. You need to evaluate what is going wrong with it, keeping in mind that it takes both of you to cause it to fail. As I've taught in this book already, the only person you can change is yourself. So, take a quiet moment when you feel peaceful and are alone and review a recent argument you had with your mother or father from your parent's side only. Take a moment to step into their shoes and feel where they might have been coming from during that altercation. Also, think about the issues they might have in their life that could have influenced them in their interaction with you. Do they have qualities that make you both alike? Or do they have qualities that make you complete opposites? We all want good relationships with our parents. We all want them to like us, accept us as we are, approve of our choices, and praise our successes. We want our parents to be supportive, give good advice all the time and generally just be there for us every time and any time we need them. That would make them "perfect" parents, wouldn't it? How many of us have perfect parents? Zero or nearly zero. Our parents are a product of their upbringing too. They will not have all those qualities I mentioned here. Often, they will do some of these parenting skills very well, while with others they miss the mark entirely, or just struggle because of their own limitations that they brought into motherhood or fatherhood. I can tell you that 95% of parents truly try to do their very best. So, what do we do when their very best falls far short, in your perception, to what you think is ideal? You completely let go of all expectations. And you let go of these expectations without judgment or anger. This is called acceptance. If you think in math terms, when solving a geometry problem, there is what they call "givens." You must deal with the "givens" with acceptance. This is the way my mother is, and I will love and accept her just as she is. If you want her to accept you, then you must accept her too. These givens cannot be changed by you. You are the variable that can change. When you change, then the outcome will be different. If you begin to accept this person with their love and goodness as well as their flaws and limitations, you have the beginnings of a better relationship.

Next, you have to consider what's important – having a loving relationship with Mom or winning an argument that leaves you both unhappy. Try earnestly and sincerely saying I'm sorry to your parent. Then, turn on your beautiful heart with unconditional love and send it to her. True unconditional love is very hard to maintain. It requires letting go of who's right and who's wrong, and loving this person no matter how hurtful you feel they were.

You need to know that even if you decide to try these suggestions with your own parents and you see an improvement in the relationship, just know that you need to continue making the effort. It's not a one-time deal, but an ongoing process that over time will have considerable benefits as you move into adulthood and have a family of your own. The goal here with family relationships including your siblings, grandparents and any other extended family you may interact with on a regular basis is to accept all of them exactly as they are and to love them unconditionally no matter what. This section, although focused primarily on the relationship with your parents goes equally well with your siblings, and other extended family.

Friends: There are all types of friendships. Some are easy, and some are hard. Examining the hard ones makes you wonder why you are friends in the first place. Friends are most definitely part of your soul family. The dynamics of each friendship is as individual as a beautiful snowflake. No two friendships are alike. Many of them can fall into two types of relationships – karmic or soul-mate type. Soul-mate friendships are usually very supportive and nurturing relationships. This is not to say you never have a disagreement, but usually they are balanced, loving and supportive.

For the purposes of this chapter, we will focus on the other kind of friendship that's based on karma. This is a friendship that doesn't seem balanced and one person tends to dominate or seemingly mistreat the other friend. The reason for this type of friendship is for both of you to work on karma. It could be karmic debt, or a life lesson that one of both of you failed to learn from in previous lifetimes. The friendships can vary greatly as to the types of issues that you need to work on. Also, these friendships can have started when you were very young, and have grown with both of you. Do you feel you have a friend or two where your feelings get hurt often by that individual, or you are always arguing and making up, or you feel unusually aggressive emotionally towards that person and then feel guilty about your feelings if they are mean or negative? These are some of the scenarios going on in a karmic friendship. The key here is, through reading this book you can begin to examine what is going on there. Mostly you need to look inside yourself to figure out how you feel, and why you might be together as friends in the first place. Examine how this person makes you feel *most* of the time. What exactly does this person do? Does it happen publicly with others around or privately? Do they say unkind things to you that make you feel bad about yourself? Do they make fun of you, and say they are just kidding when you react negatively? Are you the aggressor or hurtful one? You need to take some time to go inside of yourself, and figure out what is going on. Ask for assistance from your guides, angels, and your God-Self through meditation or just tune in quietly alone in your room. Remember that you placed this relationship in your life when you were preparing to be born. So, now is your chance to learn from this friendship. Here are some steps to do in your journal:

1. First, you need to first assess how you are feeling when you are around this person. Do you always feel bad when you hang out with them, yet feel compelled to remain their

friend? Or is it certain situations that bring out these negative qualities between you two. So, first figure out what you are feeling. Write all of this down in your journal.

2. Next, through meditation, request for guidance from your God-Self, spirit guides and angels to assist you by shining a bright light in your mind to illuminate your thoughts as to what is the lesson is here. What might be going on that you can now take the time to fix? Write these intuitive thoughts or symbols down in your journal. It may take a few days or weeks to get answers. Don't give up if you feel you're getting nothing. Keep tuning in until you feel you are receiving intuitive information that seems new or different than what you thought on a conscious level.

3. As your third step – simultaneously, while you are doing the first two steps – take a moment to examine your feelings as the friendship is going on in real time for a few days or weeks. Then, when you get a moment, write down how you felt during that day's events in your journal. What you will begin to see will be a pattern of behavior combined or paired with a pattern of emotions. For instance, do you feel like a victim with this person? Do you always feel bad about yourself? Do they seem to always get you into trouble? Are you being your authentic self, or do you feel you have to behave a certain way to maintain the friendship? These are important questions to ask yourself. If you are thinking about these things while you are engaging with that person, you will begin to pick up what is going on.

4. Once you are enlightened to some degree on the issue, now, meditate or find some quiet time alone to again figure out what you need to do. In some cases, it may mean you

must sever the friendship with that person because it is self-destructive to you. If that is the case, be thankful for the experience and the life lesson, then bless the friendship and the person in meditation or quietly to yourself. Then kindly and respectfully let that person know that you are moving on from the friendship. You can simply say that you don't like how you feel, or who you become when you are around them, so you are moving on and that you wish them well.

If the friendship is worth repairing, then you need to sit down with that person and explain how you are feeling. There may be a point of view from their side that you wouldn't have been aware of. Letting them know how you feel can give the friendship a chance to turn around for the better. Perhaps it's a situation where you didn't have all the facts about their life and the reason for their behavior, or their deeply held insecurities about themselves. By taking the leap of faith and addressing the issues, you can perhaps not only turn the friendship around, but perhaps heal it and strengthen it.

These are just two types of examples. But there's a third scenario which could be that the problems lie within you *first*. Are you insecure about yourself? Is your self-esteem or self-confidence already low? Do you feel like you're not as smart, funny, athletic, musical, social, as your friend so you become jealous of their successes even if they didn't particularly do anything to you? Do you lash out with this friend because their natural talents and smarts make you sharply aware of your shortcomings? Do you naturally portray yourself as a martyr or a victim – creating an environment from which you can be mentally or emotionally wounded by that particular friend? Having the courage to figure out that you might be the problem can generate enormous healing and growth for you if you take the steps to learn that lesson.

I'd like to add that there will be many other situations and difficulties you have with your friends that may not be specifically included here, but these three broader scenarios should help guide you to figuring out how and what you need to do for yourself. These same tools and suggestions can also be helpful in a romantic relationship as well. These tools and activities can also be used to examine your behavior in general – especially if you are *that way* with everyone as well.

Teachers, Neighbors, Acquaintances: These are lumped together because many times these relationships are not very close, or deep. They are people you interact with on a regular basis who don't fall into the category of friend or family. Of course, a teacher can become a friend, but by and large, they usually are just in a position of educating you in a neutral environment.

People who fall into this category have a different purpose in our lives. They represent how we interact with the community. They are some of our best mirrors of what is going on inside of us. They don't have an emotional investment in us, so they just act or react to us, as we do to them. But even though we aren't in an emotionally-based relationship with them doesn't mean they aren't important in teaching us some life lessons. They often teach us some of the most important things we need to know about ourselves. Their attitude to us is usually pretty detached and neutral until we begin interacting to them in a specific way that then may cause them to react.

Yes, teachers, neighbors and peers do have their own stuff. They can be cranky, angry, judgmental, introverted, annoying, self-centered, but if you look at all of them as if they are walking around with their God-Self visible and talk to them in a compassionate way, you will have better interactions with them than other people might. Do not judge their behavior or personality traits whether good or bad, but treat them with unconditional love. That doesn't mean you "love" them like you love your family or dearest friends. It means treating people with kindness and respect. More often than not, you will get a better version of them than others might. You will also create positive energy that resonates back to them that actually has a healing benefit to both of you. Remember, when dealing with people who are neutral or strangers in your world, you never know what's going on in their personal lives, or what their self-talk may be to cause them to be the way they are.

If you have a difficult neighbor or a "mean" teacher who's not very nice to you, the best thing to do is to do the opposite of what they do. If they are truly unpleasant to be around, don't be with them any longer than you need to, but never, never send them negative vibes through judgmental or mean comments to yourself about them, or to others about them. You are simply creating more unpleasantness that not only hurts another individual, but also hurts you too.

If you have taken the time to read this book, I sense that you are very interested in improving the quality of your life; that you are interested in healing yourself and finding your way to unconditional self-love, inner peace and harmony. Healing your relationships is one of the many areas of self-healing you can do to improve the quality of your life and attract more positive situations, people and outcomes.

People lash out in anger because of fear. The emotion of fear is behind every other negative emotion. If someone is angry, it's because they are sensing a threat to them emotionally. If someone is depressed it's because they fear something in their life, or they just fear life itself. When you overcome your fear in any negative situation you will have progressed in a very wonderful way that's healing.

Now, can you see a pattern in the lessons I've brought up here in this chapter? Unconditional love for all makes all the difference in the world to our inner peace and happiness, not to mention our spiritual advancement. I'm not saying it's going to be easy to do. As human beings on earth surrounded by so much terror, sadness, greed, meanness, and cruelty, it's not easy to rise above that negativity and live in a place of joy, peace and light. Making consistent and persistent efforts to improve our relationships and ourselves will help to protect us from the barrage of negativity around us. Unconditional love is a protective barrier like no other. The reason is because it protects and keeps out all negativity, but allows love and all that's positive in to support us.

Chapter 18

Healing Yourself:
Physically, Mentally and Emotionally

In any and all spiritual journeys, processes and paths, a lot of healing takes place in many different ways and through many different forms. This chapter will focus on healing at all levels of your being – but through holistic and natural means. There's a famous quote by Hippocrates, "Healing is a matter of time, but it is also a matter of opportunity." If you truly want to heal something within your body, mind or emotions permanently, then you need to take the time to create the opportunity. To truly heal anything within yourself is to be brave and fearless. When we attempt to truly tackle the emotional or mental causes for anything going on in our bodies that is unpleasant, undesirable or painful, it is taking a leap of faith into the unknown. As you know from Sanaa's character in Part II of this book, facing the fear of the unknown takes courage. But, it's so worth it. Getting through to the other side of healing is joy, peace and unconditional self-love. That's not to say that everything we must deal with is scary and hard, but the not knowing that will come up when you choose to truly heal what hurts you can be a little unsettling.

In my experience as a healer, many times people who experienced secondary symptoms or side effects such as a rash, an emotional outburst or release didn't always choose to come back. They had difficulty recognizing that these effects were simply passing through on their way to leaving the individual's body – even when I explained to them, that this is what was happening. In order for the symptoms or emotions to leave the body, often they are momentarily re-experienced as they leave the cells of the physical body. Choosing to see your healing process all the way through and seeking assistance when needed through therapy, meditation, yoga or even just sharing your feelings with a dear friend will work far better than subjugating your feelings and stuffing them back in the drawer of your body and mind.

By the same token, many healing experiences don't need reveal themselves through the emotions, but simply just heal and release from your body. Think of a journey walking through the woods. Some parts of your path will be clear, filled with wild flowers or a refreshing water stream, and you will feel wonderful. Other parts of the path might be rather ordinary and leave you feeling neutral, and then other parts of your path may have gnarly tree branches blocking your way causing you to stumble temporarily. You might fall on a rock and hurt yourself. Do you simply stop walking through the woods, or do you go through and over the branches, rocks and forest debris in order to continue on your path anyway. It's the same with your healing journey. Choosing to stay the course to get to the other side wherever that may be is what leads to true healing and those "aha" moments of putting all the mental-emotional pieces together. Truth, understanding, insights and new perceptions are formed in our psyche and emotions that allows us to change the negative physical, emotional and mental patterns within us.

Let's look at it from another way. Whenever you had to do something new, like when you entered high school after the junior high school, everything was new and different. You had to learn to navigate the building, meet new teachers, meet new people in order to make new friends, learn the rules, the organizational system of that learning environment. You had to learn to do all of these things at the same time. It's called a learning curve. We also do this every time we start a new job somewhere.

Getting back to the example of starting a new school, it's now a few months into the school year. You don't get lost trying to find the gym, the music room or the cafeteria, and you've gotten your routine down pat. You understand the building's organizational system and you know the rules. Now your perceptions and inner knowledge of your school is changed. Learning curve is over.

It's the same with healing. When you take on the root emotional cause of your illness, there's a learning curve as well. Understanding why you are sick leads you to unknown places in your mind and emotions. Choosing to navigate this download of information through the process of healing allows you to figure out how things work. If you have an emotional or physical pattern in your body that is making you feel sick or emotionally sad – the cause can be rooted in any number of ways. In this book, we talked about karma and life lessons, reincarnation and past-life issues, how we deal with difficult people and situations in a positive fashion. Truly you can see the pattern here. The true path to spiritual advancement is through purifying and the healing of four bodies – physical, mental, emotional and etheric bodies.

Now that you have some basic understanding of what true healing is really about, here is a combination of nine modalities and activities you can do to facilitate your healing process.

Affirmations – The Power of the Spoken Word Used Positively

There are plenty of New Age books that talk about the healing power of words or what they call "affirmations." These can be as powerful as you let them be, and affirmations often work very well in combination with other healing modalities. So, what is an affirmation? An affirmation is a positive statement to heal or correct an emotional pattern in your body and to generate positive vibrations towards yourself. Perhaps you have an inner dialogue of "I'm not good enough," "I'm not lovable," "I don't deserve good things," or "I'm afraid of _____," or "I have no patience for so and so." It could also be a constant stream of negative feelings of low self-esteem, low self-confidence, constant inner anger, or depressive thoughts. Affirmations that are utilized during key times of the day or in combination with all of the other healing modalities (included in this chapter) will support your efforts to change the recording in your mind. If you change the recording in your mind, then you can begin to reset the pattern in the cells of your body. Science has discovered that all cells of the body contain emotions. There is a book by Karol K. Truman, called *Feelings Buried Alive Never Die...* This script can be a powerful healing tool for you to reverse and heal chronic negative emotions that may have also resulted in physical illnesses, symptoms or diseases. Her book will be included in the appendix as one of the recommended books.

Alaskan Research Essences/Bach Flower Remedies

These two healing remedies have been put together because they are similar in how they work in the body.

Bach Flower Remedies: These beautiful, gentle-but-powerful flower essences were developed in the early part of the 20th century by Dr. Edward Bach, an English homeopathic doctor ahead of his time. He believed and made the connection many, many years ago that our physical health is connected to our emotional state. Bach made the connection between emotions and disease and worked to find an alternative and natural homeopathic means for curing the disease or illness through healing the emotions that were the foundational cause of it. Through his work, he created 38 flower remedies. The tremendous power of these remedies comes from the vibrational activity of the flowers in these concentrated solutions. Different flowers address different emotions and root causes of illnesses. You can find a Bach Flower Remedy Practitioner now through the Internet. Information on where to go will be included in the appendix of this book. Additionally, most holistic supermarkets carry the Bach Flower Remedy line complete with basic information to guide you in making the right selection for yourself. But, truly the best way to receive the most benefit is through a practitioner. For more information on Bach Flower Remedies or to find a local practitioner, you can visit. www.bachcentre.com

Alaskan Research Essences: These essences were developed by a man named Steve Johnson in 1984 in, of course, Alaska, along with co-founder, Shabd-sangeet Khalsa. Steve was inspired by the vibrational purity of the land in Alaska. In addition to developing a wide variety of flower essences, he also developed vibrational remedies with crystals (gem stones) and environmental essences that related to a weather or environmental event or occurrence that created its own unique vibrational signature and healing effect. In addition to the single essences, the two co-founders also created several combination blends to address a wide variety of common emotional and mental stresses. This even includes combination sprays for clearing the energy in a room, yourself and your belongings. Similar to Bach Flower Remedies, these vibrational essences pack a lot of power in their subtle ability of healing us on all levels. You can visit Steve's website at www.alaskanessences.com. The website has an enormous amount of information with descriptions of the wide variety of essences, along with how to put a remedy together, and how to take it internally. This modality too, provides qualified practitioners if you feel you need guidance on making the best selection.

Both Bach Flower Remedies and Alaskan Essences work to heal the emotions through healing the vibrational disturbances or leaks in our energy fields. Once you begin using these for your healing process, illness in the physical body can begin to go away, including the emotional patterns in the cells of our bodies. The key here is sticking with it, even if you feel like you are getting sick or exhibit symptoms of illness. Think of it as a releasing of the toxins in your body. If you don't give up when you feel uncomfortable physically or emotionally, you will come through the healing experience successfully. I know, from personal experiences, that this is absolutely true.

Intention

Intention is so important in everything you do that it deserved it's own healing category. That's because "intention" is the glue that connects emotions to actions or outcomes. If your words do not match you intentions, then your words will not have any impact. If your actions don't have any heart, then that will reflect in your emotional or mental state of being. Visualization is a big part of intention. It is the engine for your intention – visually giving you what you need to stay the course and believe that what you want in your life will happen. You must remain constant and consistent with your intentions. Remember what you want may not come immediately depending on what it is you have asked for, and it may not come in the way that you thought. The universe can be very humorous, creative and unique in giving you what you want. When setting an intention, be very specific and detailed. Write your intention in your journal, then pray and visualize what you intend. Doing this everyday will give the engine the fuel it needs to help the universe manifest what you asked for. Make sure it's really what you want. The last part of intention is the belief, trust and letting go once you've set the intention. I don't mean that you stop visualizing asking for what you want until it comes. What I'm suggesting is that you don't hold on to any fears about not getting it. When you let go and let the universe help manifest what you asked for, you are trusting that all will work out in your favor. If you hold on to the fear and think thoughts such as, "I can't imagine that this will work out," or "What I'm asking for is just not possible," then you haven't let go and to let God take over. Your fear, or inability to let go to trust and belief will also reverberate as energy to the universe and anything you generate energetically complies with your wishes. Make your request, set your intention, visualize and pray for it daily, and then let go. As long as what you ask for causes no harm to anyone including yourself, and it does not clash with your divine plan, then there's no reason that it won't manifest. Asking for your teacher to get fired is not a good use of intention. Asking for your own saxophone because you love playing it so much, and you don't want to have to rent the instrument anymore is an excellent use of intention. Again, be open to how it manifests and do not try to control the process. Just let it go, and let it come.

Meditation

The best way of taking control of your own healing process without any expense is through meditation. Meditation is one of the most accessible means to healing, but like many games you may have played as a child, it's easy to learn, hard to master. The good news is, even when you don't think you were very successful in stilling your mind, you still received many benefits because of your intention. *There's that word again.* Like any exercise you might do in a gym, you need to practice to get better at controlling your thoughts. Your ego and "chatter mind" want to take over the silence you are trying to create in your stillness. Focused breathing, of course, helps to bring you back to the quiet, still center. Also, when you first begin, you might enjoy doing guided meditations to keep you on track, much like you would do if you took an exercise class with an instructor. After a while of doing guided meditations, you might begin to meditate on your own. You can start with 10 minutes of time sitting with your back straight in a chair, or on the floor with your legs crossed in "sitting pose." The key to successful meditation is a willingness to diligently commit to a regular practice of it, preferably at roughly the same time of day every day. In the beginning, you may only want to do it for 10 minutes, but as you get more comfortable stilling your mind and body, you will find you can increase to up to 30 minutes at a time.

What are the healing benefits? Well, there are plenty. First, meditating helps connect the left (analytical) side of the brain with the right (creative) side of the brain, allowing them to work together more efficiently. This generates a greater level of creativity, problem solving and flexibility of the mind – all very useful abilities for making your way in the world. The more expansive your mind, the better your clarity and perception of relationships, experiences and learning will be. Meditation is excellent for your heart health, circulatory system, nervous system, endocrine system and immune systems. People that meditate regularly generally enjoy better health than those who do not. Learning to control your thoughts, allowing more peaceful and positive energies to enter in, creates tremendous overall health to the mind, body and feelings. The more you meditate regularly, the deeper your meditation can get. This will allow you to feel the presence of your spirit guides, angels and ascended masters, thereby gaining intuitive insights and those epiphanies or "aha" moments. When you feel their presence, you will automatically feel less isolation and much more love surrounding you. You will feel less alone on a daily basis, when you take 10 to 30 minutes to connect spiritually.

Included in the book will be a few meditation scripts which you can record with your voice and use to begin a regular meditation practice. You can also do a very simple mantra to get you started, like the following: "I AM the Spirit. I AM the Light."

Saying this to yourself over and over again; going back to it if the chatter mind returns will help keep you focused. Along with everything else I've included in this chapter, meditating will synergistically enhance anything else you are doing in combination to heal yourself.

One more thing I'd like to add about meditation. Do not meditate in a dark or dim room. If you wish to attract high-level energies and beings, then you need to meditate in a lighted room. Dark rooms attract energies at a lower vibration. Your goal should be to attract angels, spirit guides, ascended masters and other higher vibrational beings to facilitate your meditation practice.

Music

Music is one of my most favorite healing tools ever! Maybe it's because my first college training was in piano performance and music composition. At one time in my life, I wanted to compose music for film. I loved the idea of creating music to accompany a movie scene or to illustrate the depth of someone's emotions in a storyline. That, however, was not in my divine plan. But, the education and the learning of music was, and I use it every single day to facilitate my mood, thought processes and background enjoyment.

So, how can music help *you* in your healing process? The key here is in finding the right music to facilitate healing, and not inflame negative feelings of anger, frustration, hurt and disappointment. As holistic healer, I used music in combination with my healing program to facilitate people's healing process. It was used to help release pent-up, old emotional baggage. It was used to bring about feelings of love for themselves, their spouses, children and others. It was used to help facilitate them taking an active stand in choosing to heal and get healthier. A wide range of music was used to create the healing environment that was needed for the person on my table. Music can assist you when you are stuck emotionally. Perhaps you are having trouble releasing an emotion that's making your body uncomfortable or painful. Music can break the logjam of emotions and move the feelings along. It's important though that you do "move along" and not get caught up in the drama of feeling bad indefinitely.

You will need to change the music up as you move yourself emotionally through a pattern to bring you towards the happy ending, just like in a movie.

Typically, music from films works very well, both music with lyrics and music without lyrics. You can create a CD or playlist for your handheld device or smartphone that combines a number of songs to bring you along a journey of healing. One warning though: Do not use music that has violent lyrics or harsh heavy metal sounds. Violent lyrics and violent music have no place in your life of peace and harmony. This type of music only fosters more anger, rage, and fear. None of which are very productive in the healing process. That's not to say never listen to heavy metal bands. Some metal bands have amazing lyrics and messages of conscience and love of humanity.

As with meditation, you can use music in this manner to enhance your healing process, to move your emotions through to a positive end or just simply create tremendous feelings of love, joy and emotional support.

Network Spinal Analysis (NSA)

This is another healing modality that was founded and created in the 1980s. Dr. Donald Epstein, a licensed chiropractor, created a holistic form of chiropractic healing called, Network Spinal Analysis. This is not your old-school back-cracking chiropractic adjustments. This is a gentle-but-powerful energetic healing modality schooled in a foundation of chiropractic education and training. There is no back-cracking in Network Spinal Analysis.

This amazing healing modality has been around for over 30 years. Again, it's a healing system that puts you, the patient, in charge, with assistance through the gentle energetic adjustments of NSA. NSA can assist in a multitude of physical health problems including difficult-to-treat conditions. NSA uses gentle precise touches to the spine that give messages to the brain to create new wellness strategies for the body. The technique is gentle, but the effect is powerful. The effect not only assists physical healing and recovery, but the processing and the releasing of emotions that go with it.

If you ask your parents to seek out an NSA professional (exclusively practiced by licensed chiropractors) for you to go to, and go in with an open mind, and a commitment to healing, the results can be profound and life-changing. When my children or I get sick from anything from a cold to stomach ache, even swimmer's ear, I take them for care to my NSA chiropractor. I may still go to my children's pediatrician for a diagnosis and guidance, but for healing care, I go to my family chiropractor. We have personally experienced the benefits of NSA, and it has had a tremendous healing impact on all of us. To help your parents find an NSA chiropractor near where you live, visit www.reorganizational.org.

Reiki

Reiki is a Japanese energy healing technique. The practitioners, through a series of attunements they receive through the four levels of training to Reiki Master, become a channel of divine healing energy. By placing the hands over the body – usually about three-six inches over the body, they can sense areas of weakness, energy leaks, tingling, and other sensations through their hands that let them know where an individual needs their healing. Reiki can be very effective in relieving stress and creating a sense of calm and peacefulness. It can also relieve illness symptoms, accelerate healing, and if you allow it, can also heal you on a mental and emotional level. Again, sometimes that healing can stir up negative feelings and you'll think the Reiki isn't working, but if you bless the negative feelings and thoughts and lovingly release them, they needn't remain with you very long.

Different Reiki Master Practitioners will have different levels of abilities and talents. Always use your intuition in selecting a

Reiki practitioner for yourself. For information about finding a Reiki Master Practitioner, you can visit www.reiki.org.

Raindrop Technique

This modality is near and dear to my heart, as this is where my main healing training has been for the last six years. The Raindrop Technique (RT) is extremely effective in healing you on all different areas of your body, mind and emotions. It is usually approached with a spiritual attitude, though there is tremendous science in the physical healing process. The combination of science and spiritual is what makes this healing modality so effective. RT was created by a man named Gary Young who learned various healing techniques that also included education from a Lakota Sioux Indian chief. Combining well-known massage techniques with science and Native American healing wisdom, a Tibetan technique called Vitaflex, and other massage techniques, Gary created the Raindrop Technique. It's a set of massage-style techniques that are applied to the bottom of the feet and on the back using nine specific therapeutic-grade essential oils. The oils are applied through a Vitaflex and feathering. The essential oils are activated through our body's natural electrical system, thereby stimulating the various organs and systems to detoxify and stimulate them to work more efficiently in bringing the body back into balance. The technique in combination with the essential oils detoxifies the body, relieves pains, and can put an individual in a meditative state while they are receiving the Raindrop. This allows for the processing of emotions or mental attitudes that may need to be released. Full benefits of RT may not always be apparent immediately following a session, but an individual can have increasingly improved results in the days that follow for up to a week.

This is an excellent modality if your body has been in poor health and you want to jumpstart your healing process. The essential oils that a qualified practitioner uses are therapeutic-grade, which means medical/healing grade. If you consider the fact that in ancient times, all medicine came from Mother Nature, through the use of herbs, plants and trees, then you can appreciate that essential oils which are also an ancient healing tool, have more relevance in healing today than ever. As more and more people begin tuning in to their spiritual natures, like yourselves, you will find that traditional medicine falls far short of what our natural bodies need.

As an aside, you can also use essential oils for everyday healing. There are qualified RT practitioners around the world who can also educate you on essential oils so you can purchase them for healing yourself. Again, encourage your parents to assist you by visiting www.raindroptraining.com for information about where to find a practitioner in your area. You can also visit www.youngliving.com for information about therapeutic-grade essential oils to purchase.

Kundalini Yoga

There are many different types of yoga available now. Yoga classes are easy to find these days which is a good thing. Take some time to investigate the different types of yoga. Some may resonate with you as being a good fit for your mind and body, and others will feel like a chore to participate in. My experience has primarily been with Kundalini yoga. I have found this form of yoga to be extremely healing, and balancing to the body. It is a very spiritual form of yoga that combines yoga moves and exercises, with mantras and prayers. It is the kind of yoga that can be experienced by any person at any age, yet it can be very rigorous and strengthening to the physical body.

Kundalini yoga was founded by an Indian Guru named Yogi Bajan when he came to the United States in 1969. In 1971, he created the Kundalini Research Institute and formalized a certification and training system for teachers all over the world.

Kundalini yoga is particularly good for balancing the

hormonal system, nervous system and circulatory system. It improves the quality of your sleep and improves your overall mental and emotional attitude. It is also very purifying and you will find that not only does it do a great job of releasing old, pent-up emotions, but it enhances and recharges your immune system too. I personally recall attending my first Kundalini yoga class with a stuffy-nosed head cold. After taking the class, I found my cold healed in just a couple of days. It accelerated the healing process in my body significantly. As with many of the offerings here in this chapter, finding a qualified Kundalini yoga instructor is important and can make the difference in your experience. The training to become an instructor is intense and thorough, but you still want to find an instructor who practices what they preach, and who lives with the right intentions.

For more information about Kundalini yoga, you can visit: www.kundaliniresearchinstitute.org. There you can find a list of trainers from around the world, and then from there tap into a local instructor with you can take a class.

Summary

As you read and review these wonderful natural and/or holistic healing modalities, you can clearly see that many of them work in combination with each other. I can personally vouch for the efficacy of all nine of them in order for me to feel comfortable recommending them to you. I understand that many of you do not have control over some of the healing choices I've offered because you are living at home with your parents, and going to school; but still take the time to talk this over with your parents, share the websites with them, and help them get educated if you feel intuitively that you would like to try the ones where you need a parent's assistance and pocketbook. If you cannot do anything more than take advantage of affirmations, music intentions and meditation, you are already doing more than most people and these four activities will most definitely facilitate healing you on many levels. The most important part of any healing is through commitment and intention. If you do not have those, then no healing system, amount of money or time will make a difference in improving your body, mind and feelings.

Personal Disclaimer: Regarding those healing modalities listed that require a qualified practitioner, these suggestions come from my personal experience and are based on my personal and professional opinion as a holistic healing practitioner. You do not need to limit yourself to just these. There are many, many other healing modalities available that may be very beneficial to teens and young adults. But, not all of them would be appropriate for a teen, so it is important to do this with your parents' guidance and approval.

Chapter 19

Your Journey Begins

Although this chapter concludes the book, truly your journey is just beginning. No matter what your life has been like up to this point, be thrilled, excited and joyful because you have so much to look forward to. Your journey is just starting and it's my hope that this book can be your first GPS system to provide you with the means to take your journey and find your way.

The underlying theme of this entire book is about the power of unconditional love. That is the foundation of everything you want to build in your life. Without it, you stumble, crumble and die. Living in unconditional love though is joyful, peaceful, abundant, and successful.

It's an exciting time on the planet right now. The year 2012 marked the beginning of a huge planetary transition for earth. For the next 20 years, starting from 2012, we and the planet are beginning to raise our vibrations through breaking the old paradigms, outmoded governmental systems, religious structures and the process of purification of the natural planet in order to be able to transition successfully over the next 18 years. There are many books published that have been written over the last decade from many different authors who channel and connect with the many different ascended masters, angels and other cosmic-level spiritual beings to bring us this wonderful information. I've included a couple in the appendix under the Recommended Books section.

This is such an exciting time to be alive that you should go hug your parents and thank them for having you. So many souls would like to be born on earth right now and there are only so many human beings willing and able to birth a new life. You have been blessed with this gift. Always remember that, especially when you are having bad day, month or experience. Be grateful to even have the experience; give your bad day unconditional love and move forward.

I, myself, feel blessed for being able to write this book for you and I hope it will be a reference that you can read and re-read again and again.

I wish you much love, light and peace on your journey.

Appendix

Meditation Scripts

Grounding Meditation

Take two or three deep cleansing breaths – inhale deeply, then blow it out hard, then again, inhale deeply, then blow it out hard…then one last time, inhale deeply, then blow it out hard… Imagining all the stress and negativity residing in your body is being exhaled forcefully from your body.

Now close your eyes, and begin to focus on your breath – breathing as normal. Inhale universal positive energy, and exhale toxic, negative and stagnant energy. With each breath exhalation, your body gets more relaxed and peaceful as it's relieved of this stagnant energy. If thoughts pop into your head, just let them float away as if being carried away by the wind.

Now…imagine you are a tree. It can be any kind of tree you like, oak, maple, cherry, willow, pine, etc. You can imagine you as this tree are located in a meadow, where there's lots of space and open air, nothing to block this tree's access to the sun.

As you become this tree, focus first on the lower part of your body; imagine your feet planted in the ground, with roots, long, long roots reaching deep into the earth's core. Imagine these roots going straight down to attach to a large and heavy boulder and wrapping around this boulder thus anchoring you to the earth. As your roots attach, reach deep into the ground, feel Mother Earth's strength and energy coursing through your body from your feet. You feel strong and supported. Now, imagine your legs and lower torso are the trunk of the tree – strong, impenetrable from outside negative forces; feel the nutrients from the earth flow through your trunk as we begin to focus on the upper part of the tree.

Now bring your focus on to your heart center – this is where your tree's branches begin...these branches are broad and wide and reach up to the sun for warmth and support. Your arms and shoulders represent the branches, strong and balanced reaching up toward the sky. Your head at the center of this tree reaching toward the sun and the sky – this part of your tree receives its nutrients from the sun, without it your tree would die. Feel the warmth and the loving and supportive energy from the sun – imagining your branches, leaves and fruit feeling the life-giving energy of the sun and universe. While at the same time, you are receiving support below from Mother Earth – life and energy is flowing in both directions in your body, cleansing, purifying, restoring and energizing. The crown of your head is open and receptive to healing and universal support from the sun and Heaven. You feel peaceful and nourished as your tree blows and flows in the wind. In this state you are open and ready to connect to the universe in the form of intuition or spiritual guidance and healing.

(From here you can continue your journey by asking and receiving intuitive advice or guidance on any issue in your life, or you may count from 10 to 1, and open your eyes as you come out of this grounding meditation feeling centered refreshed and peaceful.)

Creating Your Inner Sanctuary

Close your eyes. Begin by taking deep breaths. As you breathe, think of life moving in and out of your body. Your breath refreshes and recharges your space and all your energy systems. It brings your spirit back into your body.

Take slow, deep breaths and fill your belly with that breath. Focus only on your breath. Breathe in fresh, clean air, and hold it for a count of four, then breathe out through your mouth to a count of four. As you do, imagine all the tension and strains of the day leaving your body. When thoughts pop up in your mind, let them go as you continue to concentrate on your breathing.

Now, we are going to create and build a sacred and safe place for you and your spirit to visit whenever you want.

You can design it with as much creativity as possible. You are limited only by your imagination. Keep breathing softly...

Okay, now imagine where your sanctuary might be. It could be a garden...a beach...a meadow...a rain forest. Perhaps your sanctuary is a park where you see a playground. Maybe you found a spot on the grass under a big old shady tree. There may be a brook nearby and you can hear the sound of water trickling down the pebbles and stones. You might envision different flowers...and not only see them, but smell them.

Your sanctuary might be at the seashore or on the banks of a river. Visualize your special place on the sand or on a grassy field. As you relax in this sacred space, the water seems so inviting, soothing and tranquil, and you feel completely calm and at peace listening to it.

Perhaps you have chosen a meadow or a cabin on a mountaintop as your inner sanctuary. From a vantage point high up, you can see for miles. There may be snowcapped vistas under an endless clear blue sky. Experience the world from this amazing view. Enjoy the scent of clean mountain air that is so invigorating and refreshing.

Smell the smells of your sanctuary, like the salt air of the beach, or the moist and fragrant smell of a rain forest...the crisp, clean smell of a mountain top...the smell of pine and other trees in a forest...the smell of flowers... As you smell, take another deep breath and relax even more in your special place.

Whatever your sanctuary, make sure that is feels natural and good to you.

Turn your attention to the area around the heart. This is your center of unconditional love. See this area being filled by a beautiful pink light of love. This is where your spirit lives. The healing light of love is clearing out any hurt feelings, any sadness, frustration, and anger. In its place, continue to let this beautiful pink light of love and peace and joy fill the space. Let this center fill with as much healing energy as you can possibly imagine. You are soooooo happy and peaceful in this special, sacred space.

Okay, now look around your space... See if any spirit animals have come to visit. It doesn't matter what kind of animal it is, or if it belongs in your type of habitat. This power animal has come to visit you and bring a special message for you. Look around, and see if you can spot it. This animal is one of your guides and will help you in your life here on earth. Continue breathing softly, and take a moment to listen to the message_____

_____

(Allow a few minutes to interact with your Power Animal before moving on.)

Okay...now allow your spirit animal to leave for the moment, and return your focus on your breathing. Continue breathing softly and peacefully. As we begin to awaken, start wiggling your fingers and toes as you become more aware of your surroundings. Place your hands over your eyes. While your hands remain over your eyes, open your eyes. Return to your surroundings, and when I count to three, you will take your hands away and you are back in this room...

(You may also use this sanctuary to communicate with your spirit guides and angels in the same manner.)

Meditation to Meet Your Spirit Guides

Take two or three deep cleansing breaths – inhale deeply, then blow it out hard, then again, inhale deeply, then blow it out hard...then one last time, inhale deeply, then blow it out hard... Imagining all the stress and negativity residing in your body is being exhaled forcefully from your body.

Now close your eyes, and begin to focus on your breath – breathing as normal. Inhale universal positive energy, and exhale toxic, negative and stagnant energy. With each breath exhalation, your body gets more relaxed and peaceful as it's relieved of this stagnant energy. If thoughts pop into your head, just let them float away as if being carried away by the wind.

You can begin now to visualize yourself in a beautiful forest. Take a moment to enjoy the forest. Smell the aromas of the pine trees and the fragrance of the earth and flowers. What are the colors of the wildflowers in your forest? Do you see any woodland animals? Deer....Rabbits...Chipmunks...Birds... Take a moment to look around you and enjoy the scenery and forest activity. Feel the sense of peace while listening to the rustling leaves of the trees as a gentle breeze blows over your face and body.

Now imagine that where you are standing, a huge ray of sunlight is over you, warming and nourishing you. Enjoy the feeling, and breathe in the energy of that sunlight. Imagine it is pouring it's glowing radiance through the top of your head and into your entire body – spreading peace, divine love, and healing through your circulatory system – reaching every cell in your body. Picture yourself as radiantly light and peaceful. Enjoy this feeling for a moment as you continue to breathe in this divinely energized sunlight. When you feel your entire body is completely nourished from this beautiful sunlight, begin to look around for Archangel Michael. He will appear to you and be your companion for your journey through the woods to meet your spirit guides. You can begin to greet him in any way that feels comfortable. A hug. A touch of your hand to his. A loving look into his eyes. Whatever feels comfortable. Know that you are safe, protected and loved during this journey.

Now, you will see a path through the forest. Get onto the path with Archangel Michael as this path will lead you to a clearing. Feel the loving and supportive energy of Archangel Michael as you walk. He is fortifying your courage, strength and inner self-love. Feel this energy circulating in your body as you walk this path.

You've now reached the clearing and upon this open land is a house. Archangel Michael will stay behind at the forest's edge. You do not need him as you will be within the safety and love of your spirit guides. This is the house where your spirit guides will meet you. Take notice of this house...the color, the style, the size. Look at the front door. What color is it? Is it modern-looking, ancient and old, colorful, a door from an old culture? Now, knock on the door.

Now...see who greets you when the door opens. Slowly take in the details of this individual. Is it a male or a female? What is he or she wearing? Notice the style of dress? Look at the shoes. Enjoy this moment, as you have just met your master spirit guide. Ask him or her for their name. Enjoy this moment as she/he greets you and invites you into the house.

Your master guide will now bring you into a sitting room or living room to spend time with you. Be seated, and enjoy the ambiance and décor of the room. The style, color and décor of the house and rooms are created by you for your inner peace and enjoyment. Perhaps the color is a healing color for you. Take note of the color of this room. Each time you visit, this room's color might change, but the house will remain the same. Take a moment to hear if your master guide has any guidance or words of wisdom you need to hear now. If you cannot "hear" what she is saying, then tune into your thoughts. It may be conveyed that way_____

_____

Now, you may ask him a question_____
and listen for the answer_____

_____

_____

Now it is time to meet your other spirit guides as your master guide invites them in. They all enter. There might be one or two, or several. Just take a moment to look at each and every one. See if they convey to you what role they play in helping you in your life right now. Some of these guides may be with you only for this part of your life, so take a moment to find out who they are

_____

_____

Now it is time to say goodbye. Take a moment now to thank your spirit guides and let them know how much you value their assistance. Your master guide will walk you back to the door you entered from. He will have a gift to give you. Open your hand to receive this gift. Take note of what it is and hold on to it as you leave. Thank your master guide now and feel free to express affection if you so choose as you bid your master guide goodbye.

Walk back to the forest edge to greet Archangel Michael. He will accompany you back to the area of the forest where you began your journey. Again, feel his loving energy as you walk through the pathway. Once you have returned to the spot where you started, it's time now to say goodbye to Archangel Michael. Be sure to thank him for supporting and protecting you during this journey and whatever else you might want to say to show your appreciation.

Now, close your eyes, and count backwards from 10 to 1 slowly and open your eyes. You will have returned to your room.

FOLLOW-UP ACTIVITY: Take time now to log your experience in your journal. If you can, honor your experience by finding a replica of the gift you received from your master guide in the meditation. If you can, you might want to purchase or acquire a special box for your journal and/or symbolic gifts. You can use this meditation anytime you like. The house where your spirit guides reside will usually remain the same. Also, you always want to invite Archangel Michael for protection when you do this journey.

References

King, Godfre Ray. *The Magic Presence*, Chicago, IL: Saint Germain Press. 1935

Prophet, Mark L. and Elizabeth. *The Masters and Their Retreats*. Gardiner, MT: Summit University Press. 2003

Recommended Books for Further Reading

Children of the Stars, by Nikki Pattillo – This book is written with parents in mind, but since the information is about the New Age children, there's a lot in there that you will be able to learn and relate to. It talks about the arrival of the Indigo, Crystal, and Rainbow children, their purpose on earth, and what's to come.

Feelings Buried Alive Never Die… , by Karol K Truman – This book is excellent for healing the causes physically, emotionally and mentally of emotional patterns that are hidden or stuck in the cells of the body. It's the book from where "the script" referenced in Part III came from. The book is very readable.

Karma and Reincarnation, by Elizabeth Clare Prophet – This book clearly explains these concepts and may provide you with further insights beyond what I've shared in this book.

The Magic Presence, by Godfre Ray King – This radiant book is a touching story of four teenagers during the 1930s and their spiritual journey to enlightenment and ascension. It contains a lot of spiritual teachings interlaced into this amazing story, that will radiate much spiritual knowledge and insight that you can incorporate into your life now and always.

Meet Your Guides and Trust Your Vibes, by Sonia Choquette – The first of these two books is a wonderful book to assist you in understanding the nature and purpose of spirit guides. The second book teaches further how to develop your intuitive skills. It's a very easy and readable book with exercises and tools that anyone can use.

The Omnivore's Dilemma (Young Adult Edition), by Michael Pollan – If you truly want to understand what is happening with our food, the author divides this book into three sections. These three sections relate to the three different ways food gets to our table, industrial agriculture, mass-market organic and one single farmer who works with animals and the land the way nature had intended. This edition was specifically edited for teens and young adults, so it's easy to follow and learn from.

Peace Pilgrim, Compiled by Her Friends – Peace Pilgrim lived in a constant state of unconditional love. Although I'm not suggesting that we live as simply and sparsely as she did. She exemplifies that in any situation you encounter, if you approach people and events from the place of unconditional love, you can effect great changes in people and communities. She's one of the most amazing role models that ever lived.

Soul Speak – The Language of Your Body, by Julia Cannon – This book methodically discusses the emotional root causes of many of our illnesses from the very common to life-threatening. It's written in simple terminology that anyone and everyone can read, and understand.

About the Author

Deneen Vukelic lives in Long Island, NY with her husband and three sons. She has been a holistic healing practitioner and intuitive since 2008. She is trained in Reiki, Raindrop Technique, Vibrational Raindrop Technique, Six Sensory – Intuitive Development (through training with Sonia Choquette) and has a BS in Natural Health. She is knowledgeable and trained in the use of therapeutic-grade essential oils for healing our bodies naturally, and has solid working knowledge of nutrition through the extensive research she has done on creating health with healing foods. She has been working with kids since 2010 when she began her workshops teaching children how to meditate and develop their intuition.

It was a natural next step to turn her knowledge and passion for healing and spirituality into a book. This is just the beginning. It is her hope to continue writing books for you, and your input will be very valuable. She is also in the process of developing weekend workshop retreats created specifically for teens.

Please feel free to email her and let her know what you would like to learn about in subsequent volumes. She has two more books in concept stage, but would really like your input. You can write to Deneen directly at soaringspiritualteens@gmail.com, or "like" her on Facebook, Soaring Deneen; follow her on Twitter @soaringdeneen. You can also visit her website at www.soaring spiritualteens.com for updates on new books, public appearances, workshops, etc.

Soul Rocks is a fresh list that takes the search for soul and spirit mainstream. Chick-lit, young adult, cult, fashionable fiction & non-fiction with a fierce twist.